STATUE IN SEARCH
OF A PEDESTAL

STATUE
IN SEARCH
OF A PEDESTAL

A Biography of the
Marquis de Lafayette

NOEL B. GERSON

DODD, MEAD & COMPANY · NEW YORK

Library of Congress Cataloging in Publication Data

Gerson, Noel Bertram, date
    Statue in search of a pedestal: A biography of the
Marquis de Lafayette.

    Bibliography: p.
    Includes index.
    1. Lafayette, Marie Joseph Paul Yves Roch Gilbert du
Motier, Marquis de, 1757–1834. I. Title.
DC146.L2G47   944.04'092'4. [B]   76–18118
ISBN 0–396–07341–7

FOR ANNE WENDY BRENNAN

Introduction

EVERY AMERICAN schoolchild knows that a teenaged French nobleman named Gilbert de Lafayette came to the United States during the War of Independence, fought with vigor and skill for the cause of freedom, and became a folk hero. Few people know anything more about him.

The facts are startling. At twenty the Marquis, as he was called to the end of his days in his second homeland, was a volunteer major general of the Continental line, serving at his own expense. He fought brilliantly in spite of a conspicuous lack of military experience, covered himself with glory, and was largely responsible for the American victory at Yorktown, the last major battle of the war.

Thanks to his efforts, the infant United States signed an effective peace treaty with the most powerful Indian tribes of the East.

One of the wealthiest of Frenchmen, he exhausted three fortunes in the cause of liberty.

He was one of the fathers of the French Revolution, but

risked his own life to save those of Louis XVI and Marie Antoinette. One day he was lieutenant general of France, the next a helpless, impoverished prisoner who spent five years in cells. Incidentally, he gave France her red, white, and blue Tricolor

Lafayette and his wife, Adrienne, were passionately devoted to each other, and she—along with their two young daughters —voluntarily joined him in prison for two years. The hardships she suffered there led to her early death, and for the rest of his own long life her husband venerated her memory.

His devotion to her did not prevent this eighteenth-century gentleman from engaging in affairs with two of the greatest beauties of the age. One happened to be the mistress of the future Charles X, who forever after hated Lafayette. The second was Mme de Lafayette's closest friend, and this understanding wife not only tolerated the affair but encouraged her children to treat the lady as their aunt.

Lafayette was the only man in Europe who literally defied the all-powerful Napoleon Bonaparte to his face year after year —and got away with it.

The founder of the French National Guard and twice the most influential man in the country, both in his twenties and in his seventies, he could have been president of a republic. Instead he chose the role of kingmaker and placed Louis Philippe on the throne.

He, more than any other man, was responsible for the restoration of the rights of French Protestants. Almost single-handed he ended slavery in the French colonies. He was one of the first advocates of the universal franchise and universal free education. He spent his whole adult life fighting for freedom of the press, and was an early advocate of free trade among nations. That he took these advanced positions is astonishing in the light of his aristocratic, limited background.

As an old man Lafayette became the center of an international "conspiracy" that wanted to bring freedom to Greece, Germany, Italy, Portugal, the Netherlands, Spain, Poland, and the emerging nations of Latin America. He was a hero to Thomas Jefferson, Charles James Fox, and Lord Byron. Simón Bolívar called him "Master."

A serious farmer, Lafayette introduced modern fertilization methods to France. He may have been the first to import merino sheep, as well as various breeds of cattle and hogs. He was the first to grow American corn and tobacco in France.

His personal courage was amazing, and he had a penchant for facing howling mobs alone. On the other hand, no man was more frank in seeking and appreciating the cheers of the multitude. Yet he could endure prolonged public disfavor with quiet stoicism.

He won so many laurels that honors meant no more to him than money, which he failed to understand. He thrived exclusively on liberty—and applause.

STATUE IN SEARCH
OF A PEDESTAL

1

PROBABLY NO MAN in history was less suited by ancestry, background, or education for the dual roles of champion of democracy and defender of the personal rights of man than Marie Joseph Paul Yves Roch Gilbert du Motier, Marquis de Lafayette. In his youth he would have protested violently had he known what was in store for him, but the violent upheavals of the age in which he lived, combined with circumstance and his own stubborn integrity, cast him in a role from which he could not escape.

Certainly he fitted the part and was comfortable in it. Friends who knew him all his life insisted that for many years he was a statue in search of a pedestal. His wife, who loved him more than did the other beautiful women in his life—more, in fact, than life itself—smiled at the description and is said to have clapped her hands in approval when she first heard it. It was their joint tragedy that she died before he found his pedestal and was universally recognized in Great Britain and Europe, North America and South America as the standard bearer of liberty. His friends recognized his worth from the time he was little more than a boy, and his enemies, not the least of them Napoleon Bonaparte, had to admit he earned his laurels.

The family, which originally spelled its name La Fayette, was one of the oldest and most honorable in France. The marquis who became famous in the American and French revolutions could trace his ancestry back to at least A.D. 900, but probably never bothered. Like so many of his class, he took his lineage for granted.

One of the most renowned was the first who bore the name of Gilbert Motier de La Fayette, who commanded the French and Scottish troops that defeated the English at Baugé, served under Joan of Arc at Orléans and Patay in 1429, was a member of Charles VII's grand council, and, for reasons that remain obscure, adopted the motto "Why Not?"

Perhaps the most celebrated of the La Fayette ladies was one Louise, whose beauty called her to the attention of Louis XIII. She resisted him with ease, which was a simple matter, the son of Henri the Great being a timid man. To turn aside the advances of his omnipotent premier, Cardinal Richelieu, was not so simple, but she managed this too.

By the eighteenth century the La Fayettes were land-poor nobles living in an old château in Auvergne, in the French heartland, rarely leaving the province. For century after century the men of the family were soldiers who served their king faithfully, and many died in service. They made no known contributions to the arts, the sciences, politics, or finance. They were content to rusticate, supervise the raising of wheat, rye, and grapes on their farmlands, go to war, and die.

An exception was the future hero's father, Michel Louis Christophe Roch Gilbert, who was sent off to Paris as a boy in 1743. There, in 1754, he married Julie de La Rivière, a beautiful heiress whose family had close connections at the court of Louis XV.

The young couple promptly went to Chavaniac, the old family estate, where they settled in with relatives after the fashion approved by French nobility. If the bride was treated with greater courtesy than was ordinarily extended to a girl in her position, it was because the entire La Fayette family knew that someday she would inherit an enormous fortune. Her young husband, thanks to the influence of her relatives, was granted a commission he badly wanted in the crack grenadier regiment.

In April 1757, thanks to yet another war between France and Great Britain, Colonel the Marquis de La Fayette was compelled to take leave of his pregnant wife and join his regiment. Their son was born on September 6, 1757, at the Château Chavaniac, and the court circular announced the arrival in the world of the Most High and Powerful Seigneur Marie Joseph Paul Yves Roch Gilbert du Motier de La Fayette. The baby, called Gilbert, did not set eyes on his father for several months, the Colonel being too busy training his regiment.

In 1758 the father did manage to pay several prolonged visits to Chavaniac, and when he returned to the field he corresponded regularly with his wife. He wrote about his regiment, she about their child. Neither seemed to spark to the interests of the other.

On August 1, 1759, at Minden, the Colonel led his troops against a combined British-German force, it being an old family custom for La Fayettes always to be in the vanguard of a battle. An English cannonball tore off his head, and his son, not quite two years of age, succeeded to his title.

Through his very long life Gilbert, Marquis de Lafayette, as he came to spell his name, worshiped the memory of the father he had never really known and could not remember. The men of the family were exceptionally tall, most of them standing six feet in an era when the majority of their contemporaries were at least six inches shorter. So it has been suggested, even by Lafayette himself, that the close affection he felt less than two decades later for Major General George Washington, the American commander in chief, was aroused at least in part by Washington's towering height.

The fatherless child was left in a household of women, which was dominated, as Lafayette himself later wrote, by his grandmother. The elder marquise was an iron-willed woman, accustomed to obedience in all things, and her daughters were like her. Charlotte de Chavaniac, the elder, moved in with her mother after the death of her husband. The younger daughter was considered the banking genius of the family and managed the fortune that Gilbert inherited from his father, via his mother.

The Colonel's widow spent her summers with her child at Chavaniac, but spent the rest of the year with her own parents and grandfather at Versailles, the royal seat of power. She was not being negligent in absenting herself from her son; on the contrary, it was regarded as her primary duty to look after his estates and other properties at the King's court. The fact that she was escaping the attentions of three domineering La Fayette women was irrelevant, and it made good sense for a lovely, wealthy widow to be living at court, where she would meet prominent bachelors and widowers.

Not that the Marquise was interested in men. On the contrary, as her son wrote years later, she turned to religion with such fervor that she thought of becoming a nun, much to the horror of her relatives. During her husband's lifetime she had been flirtatious and frivolous, but her whole nature changed

4

when he was killed, and her son remembered her as a charming but somber woman.

The lonely boy had one companion, a cousin, the daughter of Mme de Chavaniac, who was one year his senior. They grew up as brother and sister, and were devoted to each other. Married at an early age, the Marquise d'Abos died in childbirth during Lafayette's first expedition to America.

Males who bore the family name were expected to be valorous above all, and the good ladies of the household saw to it that the little boy left in their charge heard in detail about the exploits of his gallant ancestors. At mealtimes he was regaled with an account of what one or another of his forebears did at one battle or another, and there were so many brave La Fayettes who fought in so many battles that the child could not keep them straight in his mind.

He required a formal education, of course, and at the age of five he was placed in the care of a Jesuit priest who managed to instill in him the principle, extraordinary in a nobleman of his class, that intellect and principle were of greater value than battlefield courage. Over the years the young Lafayette sometimes forgot this lesson, but it nevertheless lingered in his mind and came to the forefront when his situation demanded a display of sustained moral courage. If any one person was responsible for Lafayette's breaking out of the mold in which he was cast, it well may have been the anonymous Jesuit.

When the boy was seven the Jesuits were expelled from France, the crown finding it convenient to blame them for the nation's political and military woes. So the child's formal education was entrusted to an abbé named Fayon, who made his own inadvertent contribution to the development of the future great man. The Abbé Fayon, as Lafayette later wrote, was a stickler for punctuation, spelling, literature, and mathematics.

He believed it essential for a nobleman to learn some language other than his own, and as he himself knew English, he taught it to the boy, even though he was a pronounced Anglophobe.

Fayon, as it happened, was a man of many violent prejudices, and he did his best to pass them along to his pupil. As it happened, however, the young Marquis—who, like most children, had to rebel against someone—turned against the ideas of his tutor. The blacks, Fayon believed, were members of an inferior race, and were properly enslaved; Lafayette went through life believing blacks were the equal of whites and deserved freedom. Voltaire, Fayon said, had been an antichrist who should have been burned at the stake. Lafayette read all the works of Voltaire that he could find, and became convinced that freedom of the press, religion, and assemblage were rights that belonged to all people and could not rightly be taken from them by any government. The Abbé Fayon never knew how much he contributed to the world of freedom.

Although young Lafayette would come into large sums of money when he reached his majority, he was not yet wealthy in his own right, and was obliged to live on a military pension paid him by the crown, a paltry sum. He was always conscious of his obligations, and wore his Sunday best whenever he rode into Chavaniac, where he confounded his grandmother and aunts by dismounting and discussing crops with the peasants who rented their property from the family.

According to an anecdote that may be apocryphal, on one occasion the ladies asked him why he defied them by talking to the farmers about their produce. "Because I care," he is supposed to have said. "When they have crops, we do well, too. When they starve, then we will starve."

When Lafayette was eleven, in 1868, his mother unexpectedly plucked him from the nest at Chavaniac and took him off to Paris to live. He had not yet been told of the great fortune he would inherit, and hence had no idea that his mother wanted to prepare him for the day when he would be required to manage his own affairs. All the excited boy knew was that he was entered as a student at the Collège du Plessis, and was enlisted in the regiment of King's Musketeers that his grandfather had commanded.

Gilbert de Lafayette had entered his natural element, and took to it without hesitation. He led his class in Latin, Greek, English, and rhetoric. Country living had made him a first-rate horseman, and he was promoted to an advanced class. His fencing master said he had never taught a more apt pupil.

Apparently the boy was a natural leader. He settled the disputes that arose between contemporaries, and was always the center of attention in a crowd. On one occasion, given an afternoon of leisure, he and several friends were threatened by a gang of toughs on the street. Lafayette coolly held his ground, and at his command all of his friends drew their swords with true military precision. The thugs fled.

The boy was no paragon, however, sometimes getting into trouble with his instructors because of his overconfidence, and certainly his sense of humor was unorthodox. According to his own account, one professor directed his class to prepare an essay on the subject of a perfectly trained horse, one that became obedient at the mere sight of the rider's whip. Others in the class went to work at once, writing furiously. Lafayette, however, lazily drew a cartoon, which he handed to the professor without comment. It showed the "perfectly trained" horse bucking violently and throwing the rider at the first glimpse of the whip.

Some teachers might have punished a student for this attitude, but the professor laughed, obviously realizing that the country boy knew horses far better than did a pedant seated behind a desk in a Paris school. The professor remained Lafayette's friend for many years, and frequently reminded him of the incident. Gilbert himself drew no moral from the story, but allowed it to teach its own lesson.

When Gilbert de Lafayette was thirteen, in 1770, his mother died unexpectedly after a brief illness. His grief for her was more than perfunctory, but her sudden passing at the age of thirty-three surprised no one in an age when the ravages of disease made heavy inroads among people of all classes. Soon thereafter his grandfather, the Marquis de La Rivière, also died, and the boy was astonished to learn that he had inherited the vast sum of almost 150,000 livres, the equivalent of some millions of dollars in the latter part of the twentieth century, as well as large estates in Brittany and Touraine.

Overnight he became one of the wealthiest of living Frenchmen, but he was not impressed by fortune, writing to his grandmother and aunts at Chavaniac that he already had everything he needed, but supposed he might buy two or three blooded horses. His great-grandfather, the elderly Comte de La Rivière, was appointed his legal guardian.

Wealth or no wealth, the boy had only one ambition in life. Like his father and all of the other La Fayettes before him, he wanted to serve in the armies of the crown against the enemies of France. His new wealth would have opened any door for him, and he could have worked toward a place of stature in the government, become a diplomat, or, like so many nobles, done nothing gracefully. But the seeds of propaganda sown by the ladies of Chavaniac had taken root and were flowering, and the old Comte de La Rivière was astonished by the intensity of his great-grandson's desire to become a soldier.

The arrangements were not difficult for the Comte to make.

Lafayette still attended the Collège du Plessis, where he would remain until he was seventeen, but the pace of his part-time military training was increased, and he was transferred to the most prestigious regiment in France, the Black Musketeers. The unit's corps of cadets, which was trained at a special military academy on the palace grounds at Versailles, was composed exclusively of the purest bluebloods. Only the sons of the nation's most powerful, wealthy, and influential aristocrats were admitted to its ranks.

So the future champion of democracy became the classmate and intimate friend of scores of aristocrats who would die on the guillotine during the French Revolution. He got along splendidly with them, and was as popular as he had been at the Collège du Plessis. He actively disliked only one of his fellow cadets, but had the good sense to keep his opinion to himself. The Comte d'Artois, grandson of King Louis XV, was arrogant, selfish, demanding, and rather stupid; in short, he was endowed with most of the Bourbon weaknesses, and his strengths, if any, were not visible to the naked eye.

Lafayette was the best rider, marksman, and swordsman in the corps, and displayed a natural talent as a leader of men on the drill field. But he was compelled, naturally, to take second place to Artois, who automatically was made captain of the cadet corps. He took care to avoid the young prince, and there was no love lost between them. This rash lack of diplomacy on the part of a boy in his mid-teens can be attributed, at least in part, to the absence of parental guidance in the orphan's affairs. But it also reveals something basic in Lafayette's nature.

For the first time in his life he was displaying the spirit of independence that would characterize him for the rest of his days. Certainly he was the product of his times and its conventions, but he never hesitated to break the rules when he wished.

He regarded Artois as unpleasant, and, refusing to curry the prince's favor, elected to ignore him. The pattern would be repeated endlessly for the next sixty years, until men everywhere, particularly those in high places, took it for granted that Lafayette would be rude to anyone who did not strike his fancy. It is significant that, even at the very beginning of his career, he was no courtier and was incapable of playing the sycophant.

By the time he entered his teens he was growing rapidly, and already stood a head taller than most of his contemporaries. He had the usual awkwardness of the adolescent, and his height, combined with his reddish hair, freckles, and candid manner, gave him something of the air of a country bumpkin. This quality was one he never lost. What most people who knew him failed to realize was that he took care to conceal his feelings behind a wall of reserve. The death of his father when he had been a baby and his long separations from his mother during his formative years left permanent scars on his personality, and many who knew him throughout his life thought of him as cold. It did not occur to them that he felt at ease only in his public postures, and that in private he was shy.

Virtually unknown and unnoticed at the court until he came into his fortune, young Lafayette immediately aroused great interest on the part of the parents of eligible daughters. None scrutinized the boy with greater care than the rich and powerful Duc d'Ayen, himself the son of the Duc de Noailles, a marshal of France. Ayen and his wife had a multiple problem: They were the parents of five daughters, and would have to scour France to find five sons-in-law of sufficient wealth and noble stature. One had already been selected for the eldest daughter, Louise. He was her cousin, the Vicomte de Noailles, son of the Duc de Mouchy, also a marshal of France.

Ayen's eye lighted on Gilbert de Lafayette as a candidate for marriage to his second daughter, Adrienne. Mme d'Ayen was scandalized, and with good cause: The girl was only twelve years old, the prospective bridegroom only fifteen. At her insistence, the plan was modified. Nothing would be said to either of the youngsters for a year and a half, a full two years would pass before the wedding, and for two years thereafter the very young bride and her adolescent husband would live with the Ayen family. Also, nothing would be allowed to interfere with Gilbert's education.

Ayen went to the Comte de La Rivière, and the necessary arrangements, including the payment of a large dowry to Gilbert, were made. It was not deemed essential to notify the boy of the matter.

Soon Lafayette began to receive invitations to dine at the Ayen home, the Hôtel de Noailles, and there he met his future wife for the first time. He and the Vicomte de Noailles engaged in stilted conversation with all five girls, the Vicomte having an advantage because he was already well acquainted with them.

For a full year.Mme d'Ayen kept young Lafayette under careful scrutiny, testing and baiting him in conversation, probing to learn what lay behind his reserve. Regardless of the formal arrangements, she did not consent to the marriage until a full year had passed.

On April 7, 1773, Gilbert de Lafayette was transferred to the Régiment de Noailles and was granted a commission as a junior lieutenant. This extraordinary development, combined with his frequent invitations to visit the Ayen family, convinced him that something was in the air, and with five daughters in the house he didn't have to tax himself to guess what was happening. He went to the Comte de La Rivière, who reluctantly told him the truth, expecting him to protest. He surprised the old man by expressing great pleasure.

Familiar with the customs of the time, he had known he would be married to someone at an early age. He regarded it as a stroke of luck that Adrienne had been chosen for him. In his opinion she was the most intelligent as well as the most attractive of the Ayen sisters; she was tall, which was a blessing, and was uncommonly pretty, with blue eyes and blonde hair.

He was unaware of the fact that Adrienne had already fallen in love with him, a fortuitous and unplanned by-product of her mother's strategy. That love never wavered, in spite of frightful hardships in the years ahead, and in time Adrienne would make sacrifices that would cause the whole civilized world to regard her, with justice, as a great romantic heroine.

Certainly she was the right wife for Gilbert de Lafayette. Her common sense and humanity, her ability to handle him, manage his finances, and give him sound advice when he needed it were in part responsible for the enduring reputation he achieved. If his ambition forged the statue of the great man, Adrienne's intellect, wit, and compassion molded it.

For six months after he learned the secret he was forbidden to reveal it to her, but in early October 1773 Mme d'Ayen told the girl what was in store for her. Adrienne was ecstatic. An hour later, through no error in maternal timing, her future husband arrived for dinner.

Her deep blush told him she knew, and he bent longer than etiquette required over her hand. Her younger sisters giggled and the adults smiled indulgently. Lafayette was outraged. The first intimacy he was exchanging with the girl who would become his wife not only was being transformed into a family scene but was being made the butt of family humor. Glaring first at Adrienne's sisters, then at her amused parents, he led his bride-to-be to an alcove choked with statuary that dated back to the reign of Louis XI.

There, away from their audience, he bent again over her hand, and then had the audacity to kiss her. If Adrienne d'Ayen had entertained any doubts regarding her seventeen-year-old cavalier, she abandoned them at that moment. For her sake he had defied convention, tradition, morality, and, most important of all, her august parents. From then until she died he was her hero, the greatest man in the world. A great many people subsequently shared her opinion, although for less personal reasons.

Mme d'Ayen did not, after all, insist on a long delay. The marriage ceremony took place in the chapel of the Hôtel de Noailles on April 11, 1774, in the presence of a small assemblage of some four hundred persons. The bridegroom was presented with a dowry of 200,000 livres. He was sixteen years old.

The bridal couple was bedded with due pomp, relatives and friends gathering around the four-poster for the ceremonial teasing that accompanied such rites. Adrienne and Gilbert lacked the patience for the sport of the guests, and proximity caused them to fall into each other's arms. The Duc d'Ayen himself hastily closed the curtains and ushered the company out of the bridal chamber.

A few months later King Louis XV died and was mourned by almost none of his subjects. He was succeeded by an amiable, slow-witted grandson, Louis XVI, who was married to one of the most controversial young women in history. Marie Antoinette, an Austrian princess, was charming and attractive, imperious and narrow-minded, flirtatious, cruel, and perhaps stupid. Her life had been so sheltered that she had no knowledge of the world beyond the confines of her palaces, and had no desire to learn.

The Noailles-Ayen clan had taken good care to be on the

best of terms with the young royal couple prior to the accession, and several were already represented in the official households of Louis and Marie Antoinette. One of the new monarch's first acts, even before the burial of his grandfather, was the approval of the purchase by Gilbert de Lafayette of a captain's commission in the Noailles dragoons.

Lafayette did not report for active duty until his seventeenth birthday, in September, at which time he was required to go to the fortress of Metz, where he would be stationed for half of each year. His duties there were not arduous; on the contrary, he had very little to occupy his time other than dine and chat with brother officers of similar noble station.

He regarded the assignment as something of a hardship because he was separated from his wife, who was already pregnant. There were many at Metz in whom he could confide, if he wished. The Marshal de Broglie, the garrison commander, was Adrienne's uncle, and his adjutant was the Vicomte de Noailles, Louise d'Ayen's bridegroom. Even Lafayette's regimental commander, the Prince de Poix, was related to the Noailles family.

During a period of several months Lafayette marched and reviewed his troops at Metz, occasionally led them on maneuvers, and spent long hours with his colleagues. He and Adrienne exchanged letters in which both proclaimed undying affection for each other. There was still time to kill.

The officers of the garrison were in great demand as dinner guests in the area. All armies throughout history having been alike, the nobles of Lorraine were on active military duty in other parts of France, and their lonely wives and daughters enjoyed the company of the gentlemen from Metz. The Vicomte de Noailles was already acquiring a specialized reputation, and had a number of conquests to his credit.

14

Lafayette had no desire to emulate his brother-in-law, but saw no harm in accepting purely social invitations to dinners and receptions. Somewhat to his surprise, he discovered that women found him attractive; apparently the idea had not occurred to him.

By this time he had reached the height of six feet and was filling out. His clumsiness had vanished, and he had acquired an almost feline grace. He was articulate, smiled easily, and had acquired the knack of devoting his full attention to a person with whom he happened to be speaking. The ladies of Lorraine found him fascinating, and the demand for his company increased. Colleagues mentioned his popularity in their letters, but he said nothing about his social life in his correspondence with Adrienne.

Whether he was unfaithful to her during this first year of their marriage has been the subject of considerable speculation, most of it on the part of French historians and all of it a waste of time. No hard evidence exists to either make or disprove a case. It is enough to say that Lafayette learned he was not lacking in charm, and did not forget the lesson.

By the time he returned to Paris late in 1774 he had acquired obvious poise, at least in the opinion of his mother-in-law. She was disappointed because he had not lost his reserve, but he was at least able to unbend in her presence.

Lafayette and his bride quickly plunged into the social life at Versailles, where the Noailles family maintained a large house near the royal palace, and during the winter of 1774–1775 they spent an average of two days each week at the court, contenting themselves with the diversions of Paris on the other days. The court, long licentious, was increasingly immersed in the depravity that, in another decade and a half, would help to spark the French Revolution.

Most people didn't misbehave out of personal wickedness, but simply followed the leader. Certainly this was what happened to that young man of principle, Gilbert de Lafayette, who had everything he wanted in life, loved his wife, and was looking forward to fatherhood.

2

THE UNIQUE SYSTEM that made the bulk of the French nobility mere appendages of the crown, a type of organization that ultimately led to the French Revolution, had come into being under Louis XIII. Brought to full flower under the Sun King, Louis XIV, the system made it necessary for most nobles to spend their entire lives at the court, where they schemed for royal favors, ignored their responsibilities to the people, and frittered away their lives.

By the time Gilbert de Lafayette came to Versailles in the winter of 1774–1775, the court had become dissolute, and only a few bothered to maintain even a facade of morality. No one remembered that France had suffered a humiliating defeat in the war with Great Britain that had ended in 1763, or that French power, long dominant in Europe, was being eclipsed by that of Britain, Prussia, and Austria. The nobles of France ate and drank to excess, danced and gambled and played, and committed adultery as a matter of course.

The shy young Lafayette was thrust into an alien world. He

and a few of his contemporaries recalled the nation's defeat and longed for the opportunity to restore French honor. The lack of principle at Versailles shocked him, and the licentiousness of the court bewildered him. But newcomers were expected to conform, and he made the effort.

He tried to play the gallant, but it was difficult for him to make small talk, and it proved impossible for him to indulge in inconsequential flattery. He had been poor for too long to enjoy gambling, and he discovered he had no aptitude for card games. He spent one entire evening drinking brandy, becoming so intoxicated that he had to be escorted home, and his self-disgust was so great that he never became drunk again.

One minor incident had lasting effects. Lafayette was a member of a group invited to the Queen's apartments to dance the quadrille, and he was too shy to tell anyone that he had never taken dancing lessons and had no idea what to do on the dance floor. Marie Antoinette laughed aloud at him.

Lafayette was deeply hurt, and never forgot the insult. He remained loyal to the crown, but entertained a low private opinion of the Queen. She, in turn, continued to regard him as an oaf. This mutual lack of trust would create problems during the Revolution, when Lafayette became responsible for the personal safety of Marie Antoinette and Louis.

Disliking court life, Lafayette nevertheless attempted to do what was expected of him. Virtually every noble at Versailles, including his father-in-law and brother-in-law, was involved in an illicit romance. So the young officer looked around, and decided to pay court to the most beautiful young woman at Versailles.

Aglae d'Hunolstein, at eighteen a few months older than her prospective suitor, had red hair, perfect features, and an amiable disposition. She was married to Comte Philippe Antoine.

d'Hunolstein, who held the rank of colonel in the army and spent most of his time with his regiment. Unfortunately for Lafayette, she already had a suitor, a member of the royal family. The Duc de Chartres, in his early twenties, was the son and heir of the Duc d'Orléans, head of the younger branch of the house of Bourbon.

It was a sensible, unwritten rule that when a royal prince showed an interest in a lady, other members of the court kept their distance from her, regardless of their inclinations. But Lafayette refused to be bound by rules he considered silly, and he actually went out of his way to create controversy. Others might be reluctant to risk royal disfavor, but he sought it by paying assiduous court to the lovely Aglae.

She was not stupid, however, and rejected Lafayette's advances, making it plain to him that she preferred the prince. Another man would have retired from the combat, but Lafayette continued to press his suit.

Nothing specific is known of Adrienne de Lafayette's reaction to her husband's attempt to establish an affair, and her situation undoubtedly was complicated by a miscarriage early in the winter. She could not have been surprised, however, and she appears to have tolerated his activities with equanimity. Men were expected to take mistresses, she had seen that her own parents were happy together in spite of her father's busy extracurricular love life, and her subsequent correspondence with Lafayette indicates that her own relationship with him remained unchanged.

Perhaps she already knew what others gradually would learn, that Lafayette hated Versailles, considered life at court a frivolous waste, and secretly longed to pursue his military career. The words stuck in his throat when he was required to flatter royalty, the ceaseless pursuit of pleasure bored him, and the dissolute atmosphere made him queasy. He was not a young man who enjoyed himself easily or who sought leisure for its own sake.

His father-in-law had no understanding of young Lafayette's emerging personality. The rules for getting ahead were rigid, and one played the game accordingly. So the Duc d'Ayen, not bothering to consult his son-in-law, made arrangements for him to take a place on the household staff of "Monsieur," the younger brother of Louis XVI, who used the title of Comte de Provence.

Lafayette was horrified. He would be a member of the inner circle and close to the seat of power, but he would also be condemned to spend the rest of his life as a courtier at Versailles. This move meant the end of his active military career.

It was impossible for him to reject the assignment, but he had no intention of accepting it, either. He found his own way to wriggle out of it. Each week a masked ball was held at the palace, which gave members of the court the opportunity to expand their love affairs without complication. The disguise worn by the Comte de Provence was transparent, members of the royal family always taking care not to hide their identity. But Lafayette pretended not to recognize him, and, deliberately picking a quarrel with him, managed to insult him. The outraged Monsieur promptly canceled the young nobleman's appointment to his staff, and the embarrassed Duc d'Ayen deemed it desirable for his son-in-law to leave Versailles without delay.

The secretly delighted Lafayette immediately returned to his regiment at Metz. There, in May, a few weeks after his arrival, he learned from a pleased Adrienne that she was pregnant again.

Contemplating his future as a father, the Marquis de Lafayette also had other matters on his mind. During the summer of 1775 he learned, perhaps for the first time, of the insurrection taking place in thirteen of Great Britain's North American colonies.

The Duke of Gloucester, a younger brother of King George III, happened to pass through Metz while on a tour of the Continent, and Marshal de Broglie gave a dinner in honor of the British prince. Gloucester, who was a Francophile, happened to be strongly opposed to the position taken by George III and his prime minister, Lord North, who were trying to compel the colonies to accept taxation.

The Americans had rebelled in April and were forming an army under the command of one George Washington, a Virginia planter. They intended to fight for their liberty, the Duke of Gloucester explained, and it appeared they were planning to try to establish an independent nation.

Lafayette and his brother-in-law, the Vicomte de Noailles, developed an immediate enthusiasm for the American cause. Steeped in the literature and history of ancient Greece, which they had studied as schoolboys, they were convinced that personal freedom was the ultimate goal of all people. And Lafayette, just returned from Versailles, was disgusted by the indifference of the French court to the needs and aspirations of the people of France. The Americans were going to create a new social order, and he wanted to help them, to join in their noble experiment.

The Comte de Broglie inadvertently encouraged the young idealists. As a soldier he saw an opportunity for France to obtain retribution for the loss of her North American colonies to Great Britain in the "Shameful Treaty" of 1763. Now was the time for France to go to war again with a distracted Britain.

In the autumn of 1775 Lafayette returned to Paris so he

would be at his wife's side during the latter stages of her confinement. He told her what was happening in America, and she shared his growing desire to help the rebels. Soon, in the privacy of the Lafayettes' suite in the Hôtel de Noailles, a small nucleus of pro-Americans was formed. The Vicomte de Noailles continued to favor the insurrectionists, and so did a close friend and contemporary of the brothers-in-law, Comte Louis Philippe de Ségur, an intellectual who had gained a thorough understanding of international affairs and who hoped the American example would bring about peaceful changes in France.

A small delegation of Americans came to Paris seeking aid from the French government. The temporary chairman was Silas Deane of Connecticut, who was in charge pending the arrival of the one American universally known and admired in Europe, the distinguished scientist, author, and diplomat Dr. Benjamin Franklin. Deane freely offered high-ranking commissions to French nobles who would join in the fight.

The Comte de Broglie conceived the idea of leading a large French army to North America, and actually began to form a staff for the purpose, recruiting a score of young nobleman along with a German soldier of fortune, Baron Johann von Kalb. The foreign minister, the Comte de Vergennes, promptly scotched the plan because France was not yet ready for another war with the British.

Gilbert de Lafayette made up his mind to cross the Atlantic and join the Americans, but he took care not to associate himself too closely with Broglie's group. He realized that his father-in-law still entertained ambitions for him at Versailles, and would prevail on King Louis to forbid him to leave the country.

In December 1775 Adrienne gave birth to a daughter, who

was named Henriette, after her grandmother. Lafayette, proud of fatherhood, took advantage of the situation to transfer himself from active duty to the military reserve. Now he could absent himself from France for a prolonged period without being guilty of desertion. With the groundwork laid, he, Noailles, and Ségur paid a number of private visits to the American mission.

Silas Deane was pleased that such prominent representatives of the French aristocracy were interested in his cause, and promised far more than he was in a position to deliver. At the very least, he told them, they would be made colonels of the Continental line; perhaps he could even obtain commissions for them as brigadier generals. These prospects were intoxicating to young captains who might have to wait a generation before they would be given senior rank in the French army.

Lafayette and Noailles told their wives the good news, and the Ayen sisters couldn't help boasting to their mother. It was difficult, too, for the eighteen-year-old Lafayette and his brother-in-law to remain silent to their friends. While their contemporaries lolled in sybaritic luxury at Versailles, they would be doing something useful with their lives, and would win glory for themselves and France.

Before long the news of the trio's plans reached Versailles, and the Comte de Vergennes became alarmed. Never would the British government believe that these prominent young men truly were volunteers traveling to America without the official sanction of the French government. Their families were requested to intervene.

Noailles and Ségur were curbed overnight because they were entirely dependent upon their fathers for funds, and the mere threat of being cut off brought them to heel. But nothing the Duc d'Ayen could say to the independently wealthy Lafayette

23

had any real influence on that stubborn young man.

The spread of the story caused snickers at Versailles. Queen Marie Antoinette may not have been responsible for the observation "I pity the Americans if they must rely on the help of Monsieur de Lafayette," but she was given credit for the remark. The furious would-be hero swore that nothing would interfere with his plans.

In the autumn, soon after Lafayette's nineteenth birthday, Adrienne knew she was pregnant again. Concern for her physical condition prompted her husband to conceal his plans from her; he may have been motivated, too, by fear that she would speak out of turn to her parents.

A number of officers were being recruited, and Lafayette sent an agent to Bordeaux to purchase a ship for their passage to the New World. Thereafter he outfitted the vessel, purchased munitions and supplies, then hired a captain and crew. His principal companion would be the German mercenary, who now called himself Baron de Kalb rather than von Kalb.

The expedition was costing the infant, hard-pressed United States nothing, and Silas Deane, in a flush of enthusiasm, gave commissions to both Lafayette and Kalb as major generals. The high rank may have been justified in the case of the latter, who had enjoyed a long military career and had actually commanded a brigade in the field. But Lafayette had never been in charge of a unit larger than a company, had never fought in a battle, heard a musket or cannon fired in earnest, or made a serious study of military tactics or strategy.

Lafayette told no one of his appointment, not even his wife, as he knew that if word leaked out an order would be issued in the name of King Louis prohibiting him from leaving the country. In spite of his precautions he was afraid the authorities might yet get wind of his plan, so he became crafty. His first step was to visit London, where the Duc d'Ayen's brother, the Marquis de Noailles, served as the French ambassador.

Adrienne's husband was given a warm reception, and Lafayette was taken to court, where he was presented to George III. No one would have imagined that a young man in his position would turn around almost overnight and take up arms against the British monarch, which was precisely why Lafayette promoted the farce. The very idea was so outrageous he found it irresistible.

He spent most of February 1777 in London, and finally received word that his ship was waiting for him. Early in March he returned to France and traveled incognito to Paris, where he spent three nights at the temporary residence of Baron de Kalb. During this time he paid secret visits to his friends Ségur and Noailles, and told them his plans.

He neither saw nor communicated with his wife, however, although he rode past the Hôtel de Noailles two or three times. His guilt was overwhelming, and he wrote a long letter to Adrienne, begging her pardon for his neglect and saying he would be unable to blame her if she refused to see or speak to him again. He hoped she would understand that his plans would be ruined if he made an appearance at her father's house.

Prior to his departure from London Lafayette had made the mistake of writing his father-in-law and confessing all to him. The furious Duc d'Ayen, who knew he was returning to France prior to sailing for the New World, went to Versailles, where Louis XVI promptly promised to issue a formal writ that would make it impossible for Lafayette to travel abroad again.

Unaware of the specific steps being taken but knowing he could not afford to tarry, Lafayette went to Bordeaux with Kalb. Their ship, *La Victoire*, was riding at anchor, and they hired a boat to take them across the harbor. As they were about to leave the dock a messenger arrived with word that the crown was issuing the dreaded order.

Not having received the formal notice, however, Lafayette went on board *La Victoire*, which sailed without delay to the little Spanish port of Los Pasajes, across the Spanish border, to await the arrival of other volunteers.

There the long arm of Versailles caught up with Lafayette, and a courier handed him the document bearing the royal seal. By command of King Louis he was forbidden to go to the New World. He was ordered to proceed without delay to Marseilles, where he would join his father-in-law for a six-month tour of Italy. Nothing could have appealed to the young marquis less than the prospect of traveling through Italy for half a year with a justifiably furious Duc d'Ayen.

He felt compelled to obey the monarch, however, and bidding Kalb an almost tearful farewell he returned to Bordeaux. The first person he encountered there was the Vicomte de Mauroy, also the recipient of a commission from Silas Deane as a major general. Mauroy told him the whole court at Versailles, including Louis XVI, actually approved of what he was doing, and that the King had signed the order only to placate the badly upset Duc d'Ayen.

By returning to Bordeaux instead of proceeding without delay to Marseilles, however, Lafayette had disobeyed a crown command, and the governor of Bordeaux felt compelled to issue an order for his arrest. This gesture tipped the scales, and impelled Lafayette openly to defy the King. He obtained a disguise—according to some accounts he dressed as a woman, although his height makes this unlikely—and slipped across the Spanish border again. Now he was a rebel who was not only thumbing his nose at his father-in-law but openly rejecting the specific authority of the monarch to whom he owed allegiance. He rejoined *La Victoire* as the ship was taking on its last supplies of water, vegetables, and fresh meat. Kalb, who had assumed he had abandoned his plans, was astonished to see him.

According to a letter Kalb wrote to his wife, Lafayette greeted him with the words "I am an outlaw. I prefer to fight for the liberty of America rather than lose my own liberty and languish in a French prison. So, my friend, we shall be comrades in arms after all."

An official court circular was issued, instructing all officers of the crown to apprehend and place under arrest the rebel who had refused to obey King Louis. Adrienne de Lafayette was disgraced, but in private she was proud of her clever, courageous husband.

The incident, which resembles a second-rate French farce, is significant in its delineation of the character of Gilbert de Lafayette. Law-abiding and loyal to the crown for all of his nineteen and one-half years, he had tried to outwit his father-in-law and seemingly had been trapped. The order for his arrest had struck him as unfair, and had sent him into open rebellion. When he believed a principle was at stake and, even more important, when he wanted his own way, Lafayette allowed nothing to stand in his path.

THE TRANSATLANTIC VOYAGE, undertaken in the middle of April 1777, was endless. Lafayette was the owner of the ship, which had cost him more than 100,000 livres, and the captain courteously offered to teach him seamanship and navigation, but he declined. Neither then nor at any later time in his life did he display even the slightest interest in the sea, and he wrote to Adrienne that he found a voyage "melancholy" because such a vast expanse of water was "sad."

He and Kalb ate most of their meals with the captain, but he rarely mingled with the fifteen or twenty junior volunteer officers on board. He exercised daily, regardless of the weather, by stalking up and down the open deck, and then retired to his cabin, where he read books on military strategy and tactics loaned to him by Kalb. He learned still more, he later declared, by rereading Caesar's *Gallic Wars* in Latin. He also wrote a running letter to his wife, adding to it every few days, the document finally reaching her at the end of the summer.

At the end of the first week in June gulls appeared overhead, indicating that land was fairly near, and on June 15 *La Victoire* dropped anchor at the mouth of a small river near Charleston, South Carolina. The captain refused to sail farther upstream without a pilot. The voyage had lasted fifty-nine days.

The area was thick with pines and other trees, the forest seemed as vast as the Atlantic Ocean had been, and there was no sign of human habitation anywhere. Lafayette, Kalb, and two junior officers continued the journey in a longboat manned by four sailors.

After rowing for several hours the party at last encountered several black slaves, and when Lafayette presented them with silver coins they offered to take the group to the nearest plantation house. They had to hack their way through the jungle-like undergrowth, and Lafayette suffered the humiliation of breaking his smallsword. At last they saw lights ahead and were greeted by a hail of bullets.

Lafayette and Kalb shouted in the best English they could command, identifying themselves, and the firing stopped. They were greeted by a Major Huger of the South Carolina militia, who opened his house to them when he learned of their mission. He had fired at them, he explained, because a whole company of German mercenaries imported by the British had deserted, and was attacking travelers and plantations in the vicinity.

Lafayette spent his first night in the New World in a feather bed, listening to the whine of mosquitos. The next morning he and Kalb ate a huge breakfast consisting of strange cereals, fruits, and barbecued meats. This was Lafayette's introduction to American hospitality, and he was so overwhelmed that he remembered the occasion for the rest of his days, often referring to it and enumerating the dishes he had been served.

Major Huger escorted him to Charleston, and a ketch was

dispatched to guide *La Victoire* to the city. Many of the aristocrats spoke French. A suite was made available at the best inn for Lafayette and Kalb, and hostesses promptly gave a series of banquets for the visitors. Any man who had purchased a ship of his own to cross the Atlantic in order to aid the American cause was necessarily a hero, and for a week Lafayette was feted, wined, and dined. State officials hailed him in speeches, officers of the hard-pressed local militia toasted him, and Charleston's prettiest girls flirted with him. He could have remained for many weeks.

He was eager to set out for Philadelphia, however, so he purchased horses and baggage carts for his entire company, which now numbered sixteen. They left Charleston on June 22, the local militia accompanying them on the first day's march.

The journey to Philadelphia required more than a month, and Lafayette became well acquainted with the vast American wilderness. Roads were few, so the company often traveled through forests or across open country. They encountered limited numbers of inns, and necessarily spent most of their nights in the open, cooking their own food. Rains were heavy, the sun was hot, and the march seemed endless to most of the French gentlemen, who soon became discouraged.

Lafayette, however, relished every moment of the journey. He had fallen in love with America, sight unseen, before coming to the New World, and he saw her through a lover's eyes. His letters to Adrienne were filled with descriptions of rivers and mountains, forests and plains. He was impressed by the absence of stone forts, and he frequently commented on the sturdy independence of the settlers, who were so unlike the cowed peasants of Europe. Occasionally he paused to hunt and fish, and he wrote to Adrienne, "The United States is the most marvelous land on earth." He clung steadfastly to that opinion as long as he lived.

The party reached Philadelphia on July 27 and, hastening to an inn, changed from their travel-stained clothes into their dress uniforms. Then they repaired to the Continental Congress, expecting immediate assignment to active military duty and prompt reimbursement for their travel expenses, as Silas Deane had explicitly promised in writing. Instead they were coldly received and told their request to aid the American cause would be studied.

Members of the Congress were not so curt as some of Lafayette's early biographers portrayed them. The truth of the matter was that they were deeply embarrassed by the unexpected arrival of fifteen Frenchmen and one German, all of them bearing supposed commissions. Silas Deane had exceeded his authority. The Congress was finding it difficult to meet the payroll of the Continental Army, and there were no funds available for the salaries of these foreign volunteers. What was more, General Washington and a number of his principal subordinates were finding that adventurers from Europe were more trouble than they were worth. Many were proving unreliable, American troops refused to serve under them, and they even quarreled among themselves.

The members of the Foreign Relations Committee who interviewed Lafayette were ill at ease. This youth of nineteen, totally lacking in combat experience, was the age of most American lieutenants, and the very idea of granting him a commission as a major general was absurd. He was thanked for his offer and politely urged to return to France.

Instead he went to his rooms at the inn and wrote a brief letter to the Continental Congress:

After the sacrifices that I have made in this cause, I have the right to ask two favors at your hands: the one is, to serve without pay, at my own expense; and the other, that I be allowed to serve at first as a volunteer in the ranks.

The unexpected offer gave the Congress pause. This extraordinary young man would cost the United States nothing. General Washington, the commander in chief, was expected in Philadelphia the following day, so a final decision was deferred pending a conference with him.

It has been said that Washington and Lafayette took to each other at first sight. Certainly they achieved a meeting of minds after a session that lasted more than an hour. Both were aristocrats, and each recognized the other as a gentleman. Washington, wise in his judgment of character, saw in the youth what no one else had yet divined, that he was a natural leader of men.

At his instigation the Congress confirmed the appointment of Lafayette as a major general, members of Washington's staff passing the word to disgruntled American officers that the newcomer's rank, for all practical purposes, was strictly honorary.

Eloquently persuasive when he had cause, the shy Lafayette persuaded Washington to grant an interview to Baron de Kalb, and sang his praises so insistently that he, too, was given a place of stature in the American military hierarchy. Kalb earned his way, and made major contributions to the American cause.

Lafayette, concerned about his status, had no way of knowing that he had become a father for the second time. On July 1 Adrienne had given birth to another daughter, who was called Anastasie Louise Pauline.

At the end of July Lafayette joined the ragged American

army in its bivouac near Philadelphia. Senior commanders and members of the staff were prepared to snub this "major general," but he disarmed them. He was modest in all things, never displaying nor referring to his own great wealth. He shared discomforts and hardships without complaint. He took care never to criticize his hosts, and even when asked for ideas regarding possible improvements, he invariably replied, "I am here to learn, not to preach or teach."

Because he was a high-ranking French nobleman he was often invited to dine at headquarters, and members of Washington's staff soon discovered he was a very pleasing companion. He quickly became friendly with Colonel Alexander Hamilton, the aide-de-camp, and other staff members. Colonel Henry Knox, the former bookseller who was the chief of artillery, said he was well read and, equally important, knew a great deal about food. Since only the plainest fare was available, Lafayette and Knox apparently amused themselves by discussing grand dishes.

Washington became fond of the young Frenchman, too, and they gradually established such a close rapport that sometimes a glance was enough as a means of communication. Years later Lafayette often referred to Washington as "my father," and Washington treated him like a son.

In these first weeks of their relationship, however, the commander in chief faced a problem. Lafayette made it clear, in a delicate way, that as a major general he was prepared to command a division as soon as one was available. But Washington had no intention of giving any such command to the foreigner, even though it was becoming evident that Lafayette's military training had been sound. For the present he was loosely attached to headquarters, informally serving the functions of an aide-de-camp until the commander in chief could decide what to do about him.

Meanwhile there were minor complications about which both Washington and Lafayette were ignorant. The French government asked Dr. Franklin, newly arrived in Paris, to insist that the Congress not grant a commission to the Duc d'Ayen's rebellious son-in-law. Franklin was in no hurry to forward the request, the Comte de Vergennes having hinted, perhaps, that the French government merely wanted the form observed and did not care about the substance. By the time the communication reached the Continental Congress it was too late, the commission already having been granted. Besides, by that time Lafayette was a genuine hero.

"The boy," as Washington habitually called him, took part in his first engagement on September 11, 1777, in what came to be called the Battle of Brandywine.

Major General Sir William Howe, the British commander, left his New York headquarters in July, sailing with a force of 15, 000 men to Chesapeake Bay. It was his intention to approach the American capital, Philadelphia, from the southwest.

He was opposed by Washington's 11,000 Continentals and militiamen at Brandywine Creek, where the Americans occupied a strong position on the heights overlooking the river. Howe feinted, sending the bulk of his troops north to a place later known as Chadds Ford, where they crossed the river.

The Americans hastily moved to a new line to oppose the Redcoats, and both of Washington's flanks promptly collapsed. His center held firm, however, which gave him the time to bring up his reserves, and although the Americans lost the battle they achieved their ultimate objective. They still blocked the road to Philadelphia, and their little army was intact, keeping alive the struggling nation's hopes.

Lafayette was given no command, and he ranged up and down the line, trying to encourage the defenders. At the climax of the battle, when the vital American center was in danger of faltering, he galloped up to the vanguard, only a few yards from the British position, and his personal example of indifference to danger rallied the hard-pressed defenders. A number of eyewitness accounts indicate that his demonstration of courage electrified and inspired the Americans, and may have been more responsible than any other factor for the stiffened resistance.

Lafayette wore his new blue-and-buff uniform of a major general of the Continental Army for the first time, and the gold epaulettes on his shoulders attracted the attention of Redcoat sharpshooters. A bullet cut through his hat without touching him, and another passed through his coat but left him unscathed. Ultimately, however, his luck deserted him, and he received a painful leg wound that forced him to retire from the field. Two weeks later he wrote to his wife:

> The ball passed through the fleshy part of the leg without touching either bone or nerve. The surgeons are amazed at the speed with which it is healing. They fall into an ecstasy each time they renew the dressings and maintain that it is one of the wonders of the world. I, for my part, think it an infernal mess, extremely tiresome and not a little painful. It is all a matter of taste. . . .

The news created a sensation in France, and there, even more than in America, Lafayette was hailed as a hero. Great Britain was the enemy, and the newspapers printed glowing accounts of the young officer's exploits. No less an authority than Benjamin Franklin said that Lafayette's conduct at Brandywine, culminating in his wound, doubled the popularity of the American cause in Paris.

Unwilling to remain idle any longer than necessary, Lafayette returned to active duty after less than three months'
convalescence, even though he limped badly and had to use a
walking stick. The Americans had gone into winter bivouac at
Valley Forge, a "natural fortress" in the Pennsylvania wilderness, and he took it for granted that he would share their lot.

The terrible 1777–1778 winter at Valley Forge is one of the
best-known sagas of the American Revolution. The army of
11,000 was inadequately fed, housed, and clothed. Men
wrapped themselves in rags, and many had no boots. Local
farmers could contribute little to them, and they survived only
by raiding British supply columns. General Washington lived
in a farmhouse, but everyone else had to sleep in makeshift
huts built partly underground. Illness was rampant, the discouraged deserted, and the men who remained suffered almost
beyond endurance.

That the wealthy young French nobleman voluntarily and
without complaint shared this ordeal stunned Americans of
every rank. The literate wrote home about him, and his fame
spread with unusual speed. Almost overnight he became one
of the most popular officers at Valley Forge, and people in all
thirteen of the new states sang his praises.

Even though he still limped, Lafayette was not content to
remain inactive through the winter, and begged for action.
After what he had done at Brandywine General Washington
believed he had earned the chance. Major General Nathanael
Greene of Rhode Island was in charge of the camp's defenses,
and Lafayette was given his own command, a force of about
three hundred men. One day in late January, while on patrol,
the unit encountered a slightly larger party of Hessian mercenaries.

The engagement that ensued was brisk and decisive. Lafayette not only attacked vigorously, but fought in the forest with the aplomb and skill of an experienced wilderness soldier. He had already demonstrated that he was an instinctive leader; now he proved that he could grasp instantly the principles and application of battle tactics under exceptionally difficult conditions. He suffered no losses, and routed the Hessians.

The victors returned to Valley Forge, and the entire camp turned out to cheer Lafayette. He had won the enthusiastic support as well as the friendship of the Americans, and they regarded him as one of them. From that time forward, for the rest of his life, he held a special place in the affections of the American people. Other foreigners, among them Kalb and Baron von Steuben, who would train the Continentals and mold them into a disciplined fighting corps when spring came to Valley Forge, were accepted. But Lafayette achieved something more, winning the undying love and gratitude of the nation he served so unselfishly.

His own attitudes had deepened. He had come to the New World craving adventure and glory, and he had won both. But his association with the Patriots had convinced him that the cause for which he was fighting was right and just, and he developed an abiding love for his second country.

General Washington applied to the Continental Congress for permission to give him a major command, and the Congress promptly obliged, giving him the right to take charge of a brigade "in recognition of the military talents of which he has just given brilliant evidence." The commander in chief, already treating him like a son, gave him his choice of units.

Several brigades petitioned for the right to be commanded by Lafayette, who was embarrassed, as he wanted to hurt no man's feelings. The unit he selected was made up, in the main,

37

of Washington's fellow Virginians, and General Lafayette immediately ordered new uniforms and boots made for the men at his own expense. The Congress, unaccustomed to such displays of generosity, was startled.

A group of Congressmen who disliked Washington tried to use the young marquis for their own purposes, and offered him command of an expedition that would invade Canada. The mere prospect of being responsible for the capture of territory that had been taken from France by Great Britain in 1763 was exhilarating, and he went off to Albany, New York, with high hopes.

It did not occur to him that his command would be independent, and when that fact finally dawned on him Lafayette wrote to the Congress, making it plain that he would take the field only under orders from General Washington. His loyalty to the commander in chief was absolute and unwavering, and as a consequence none of the troops he had been promised ever arrived. Even his Virginians were mysteriously delayed, and he returned to Valley Forge in time to take part in Baron von Steuben's rigorous training program.

In the meanwhile France was moving closer to a full alliance with the infant United States. In October 1777 the Army of the North, ostensibly commanded by Major General Horatio Gates, had won a major victory over a British corps under General John Burgoyne at Saratoga. This event convinced the French government that there was a chance the Americans actually could win their independence.

Equally important were Lafayette's exploits, which appealed to the sentiments of official France and the common people alike. Saratoga won the mind of France, but Lafayette's deeds won the nation's heart. In January 1778 the Prime Minister, the Comte de Maurepas, notified the American mission that

King Louis XVI recognized the independence of the United States. Late the following month, after news of Lafayette's victory over the Hessians reached Paris, France ordered the dispatch of a powerful fleet to the New World, ordered supplies, arms, and munitions sent to the Americans, and offered direct military aid, as well, in the event that Great Britain declared war on her.

A special messenger brought the news to Philadelphia, arriving there late in April, and hurried on to Valley Forge. The long winter of suffering had come to an end, and the promised aid of the most powerful country in Europe gave the Americans new hope. Washington publicly told Lafayette that the exploits of the young marquis had turned the tide of French public opinion.

In May 1778 a powerful French fleet commanded by a senior admiral, Comte Charles d'Estaing, sailed up the estuary of the Delaware River, and America rejoiced. Lafayette was sent as the official representative of the Continental Army to greet his fellow countrymen. He was pleased, but at the same time must have been apprehensive. In spite of his achievements in the New World he could not have forgotten that he had defied a direct order given by King Louis himself when he had left France, and for all he knew the navy had been ordered to place him under arrest and return him to Paris.

Admiral d'Estaing dispelled his fears by embracing him and telling him all France was proud of him. The Admiral carried personal letters for him, one from his father-in-law, which tacitly forgave him for disobeying the crown. There was also a letter from Adrienne which shocked and pained him: Their elder daughter, Henriette, had died suddenly after a brief illness.

Lafayette mentioned the tragedy to no one, and Washington learned of it by accident from a member of Admiral d'Estaing's staff. The commander in chief offered Lafayette a leave of absence, but the Marquis preferred to stay in America. He was needed here, he said, and his wife was surrounded by her relatives

The French sailed off to Rhode Island, where they would make their headquarters before meeting the British fleet somewhere off the New England coast. Major General John Sullivan, already in command of the army in Rhode Island, was directed to cooperate with Admiral d'Estaing, and a special corps was sent north under General Greene to augment his forces. Lafayette was made deputy commander of that corps.

Estaing arrived at Newport late in July, and from the outset he and Sullivan failed to hit it off. The Admiral was a haughty aristocrat who assumed that Sullivan had complete control of his forces and of the resources of the area. The General was cantankerous, thin-skinned, and defensive. Misunderstandings arose, unpleasant words were exchanged, and relations between the allies became strained.

Lafayette was caught in the middle, with each side not only demanding his full loyalty but expecting him to persuade the other to see reason. Lafayette the soldier was necessarily replaced by Lafayette the diplomat, and the young man, not yet twenty-one years old, was not equal to the task. Franco-American relations at Newport became even more strained.

Estaing put out to sea, where his fleet was so badly battered in a storm that, desperately needing repair, he had to return to port. Only the shipyards in Boston were large enough and sufficiently well equipped to take care of his needs. But by this time some of his hotheaded remarks about Americans had been repeated to members of the Massachusetts legislature, and General Sullivan contributed nothing to the amity of nations by repeating his opinions of the Admiral. The Massachusetts legislature refused to grant the French fleet the right to put into Boston for repairs.

Lafayette's services were urgently required, and he stepped into the breach, using all of his charm and powers of persuasion on the legislature, which changed its mind and granted permission for the repairs to be made. Sullivan continued to demand the loyalty of Lafayette, a subordinate general, and Estaing assumed the loyalty of the Marquis, a fellow Frenchman.

Lafayette was the central figure in an unfortunate tug of war. General Washington, well aware of his dilemma, strongly suggested he solve it by returning to France on a leave of absence. Lafayette was on the verge of accepting, but a rumor reached Boston that a major invasion of Canada was being planned. He wrote at once to the commander in chief, requesting that he be given the corps that would make the march.

Washington's reply was frank. He knew of no such expedition, he said, and the United States was not yet strong enough to undertake such a campaign. He advised Lafayette to take his leave, saying the holiday would not interfere with his command of an expedition in the event that one should be planned at some future time.

The Continental Congress passed a special resolution granting a leave of absence to Major General Lafayette, to be terminated at a time convenient to him. He was thanked for his services to date, and the American minister at Versailles was directed to present him with "an elegant sword, with proper devices."

The French minister to the United States, Gérard, wrote to the Comte de Vergennes that Lafayette was "the idol of Congress, of the army and of the people of America." The observation may have been a slight exaggeration, but in essence it was true.

As a final gesture the Congress put a ship at Lafayette's

disposal for his voyage, naming it *L'Alliance*. He sailed late in 1778, with no one in France aware that he was coming home. He carried special messages from the Congress to Prime Minister Maurepas, as well as confidential dispatches to the United States mission in Paris. Landing at Brest on February 6, 1779, he went straight to Versailles to pay his respects to King Louis.

He was received by the Comte de Maurepas, who congratulated him on behalf of France—and then, as symbolic punishment for having defied the crown, ordered him to proceed directly to Paris without being received in audience by Louis XVI. He was directed to confine himself to the Hôtel de Noailles for a period of ten days, and to receive no one but relatives during this time.

Lafayette's official welcome was merely being postponed, as he well knew, and in the meantime he would enjoy an uninterrupted holiday with his family. He accepted the mild rebuke in high spirits, and, still wearing his American uniform, to which he had added the Bourbon sash across his chest, he set off to surprise his wife.

ADRIENNE DE LAFAYETTE was ecstatic. After a separation of two years she had her husband all to herself for a week and a half. It was true she had to share him with the rest of the family at dinner and supper, and that his former comrades Noailles and Ségur plied him with endless questions about his exploits in the New World. Even her father treated him as an equal now and wanted to know many things about the unusual new American form of government. But husband and wife spent most of their time in their own suite, and Lafayette had the opportunity to become acquainted with little Anastasie, whom he had never seen before.

Not yet twenty-two, Lafayette had changed, as Adrienne wrote to his aunts at Chavaniac. He had been shy and gangling when he had gone off to America, and in the presence of his elders he had been deferential and reserved. That period of his life had come to an end. Now he was a man hardened by battle and suffering, an authentic hero who had earned his spurs as a major general. More than any other man he was responsible

43

for the alliance between the United States and France, and General Washington had told him in private of the contents of one communication sent by the Continental Congress to the French government: It was suggested that a joint invasion of Canada be undertaken, and that Lafayette be given command of the combined Franco-American armies.

Self-assured and jaunty, the Marquis spoke firmly about matters on which he had become an authority. He was still modest when asked about his exploits, but he bowed his head to no one. He was deservedly famous as well as wealthy, he discussed military matters with the old marshal, the Duc de Noailles, and he displayed no uneasiness in the presence of his father-in-law. Best of all, in Adrienne's opinion, was his consistently tender, considerate treatment of her in all things.

What Lafayette did not yet know was that Aglae d'Hunolstein had taken note of his renown and, bored by the attentions of frivolous nobles at Versailles, was sorry she had spurned him. Other girls, younger and perhaps equally attractive, were becoming centers of attention, and she confided to intimates that through Lafayette she could recapture the limelight. She had every intention of renewing her acquaintance with him, and had an open mind as to where it might lead.

During his ten-day incarceration Lafayette had a taste of the adulation that awaited him. He was forbidden to receive visitors, but scores of high-ranking nobles left their calling cards. Adrienne received a letter from the elderly Voltaire, congratulating her on her marriage to a man who had become the symbol of human liberty. Huge crowds gathered outside the Hôtel de Noailles each day, and in order to disperse them he had to make repeated appearances on a balcony.

The Duc d'Ayen helped his son-in-law compose a carefully worded apology to the crown, a difficult task at best. Regardless of the policies of the French government, which had become decidedly pro-American, King Louis never forgot personal insults, and the marquis who had become the idol of America and captured the imagination of Paris certainly had insulted him. Although affable in most things, Louis was known to carry grudges, and there was no way of guessing how he might react.

At the end of the ten days of confinement Lafayette went to Versailles, entering the grand Hall of Mirrors with a radiant Adrienne on his arm. Her nervous father and grandfather hovered in the background. Her own attitude was plain: Whatever her husband's fate might be, she intended to share it.

Louis XVI arose from his chair and, in the presence of the entire court, embraced Major General the Marquis Gilbert de Lafayette. To the surprise of those who knew her, the Queen also kissed him, and scores of ladies followed her example.

The Comte de Maurepas rescued Lafayette and carried him off to a meeting of the Cabinet, which was held behind closed doors and lasted for several hours. Thereafter he met daily with one or more of the ministers, and was influential in the making of the plans for future Franco-American operations.

Louis XVI was pleased to assign a suite of rooms to Lafayette, who was obliged to live at Versailles for a time. Adrienne spent one or two nights there each week, but preferred to retire to the infinitely more comfortable and less crowded Hôtel de Noailles, nearby. She shared the view of many nobles that the quarters in which even royal favorites were compelled to live at Versailles were far more cramped than were servants' rooms elsewhere.

Thanks to the direct intervention of Marie Antoinette, who at this period of her life was not slow to enhance her own popularity at court by espousing the cause of a hero, Lafayette was able to purchase the command of the King's Dragoons, a crack cavalry regiment, from the Marquis de Créquy. He had to pay 80,000 livres, a considerable sum, but was now a full colonel in the French army. As he had not yet reached his twenty-second birthday, a number of nobles who held lower ranks in the military were jealous of him.

Many of them held the Queen directly responsible, and it was inevitable that rumors about her and Lafayette should circulate both at the court and in Paris. These stories were completely untrue. Marie Antoinette recognized Lafayette's worth to the crown, but she cared no more for him now than she had when she had laughed at him for being a clumsy oaf, and at no time did she receive him alone in her private apartments or elsewhere.

Whenever Lafayette appeared on the streets of Paris he was followed by large crowds and applauded. He received a standing ovation when he and Adrienne attended a play at the Comédie Française, and he was surrounded when he went to a coffeehouse with friends. In the hope of recapturing some measure of privacy, he stopped wearing his uniform and appeared in public in civilian clothes, but still he was recognized.

At Versailles he saw Aglae d'Hunolstein almost daily, and she indicated her interest in him, but had to be subtle about it. She was still the official mistress of the Duc de Chartres, and His Royal Highness was already showing a lively jealousy of the conquering hero. Aglae was required to exercise discretion, to be sure, as not even the most beautiful woman in France could afford to cheat on a royal prince with impunity.

Lafayette had demonstrated that he was impervious to British bullets, but he succumbed to Aglae d'Hunolstein's charms. Following the conventions of the times, they professed to be "in love" with each other; many couples engaged in illicit romances maintained the same polite fiction. Lafayette continued to sleep with his wife, who was again pregnant, and he could meet Aglae only with difficulty. Literally nothing is known about their occasional meeting places.

Posterity cannot regard Lafayette's association with the lovely Aglae as a serious interlude in his life. Other men who were interested in her at one time or another wrote, independently of each other, that she cared only for herself, using her lovers "as adornments."

Lafayette had little time for love, marital or illicit. He was called into daily meetings by the Comte de Vergennes, and he was seen entering and leaving the War Ministry in Paris with great frequency. It was obvious that he was playing a major role in the planning of a military campaign against the British, but he discussed his activities with no one. When asked, he merely smiled and said, "I have given the Comte de Maurepas my word not to talk about these things."

The most efficient Austrian secret agent in France was Marie Antoinette, who wrote regularly to her mother, the Empress Maria Theresa, about everything of consequence that she gleaned. The Queen developed a lively interest in Lafayette's activities, and, summoning him one day, inquired about them. He replied as he did to others, and Marie Antoinette was furious. It was said that she never forgave his impertinence.

Late in the spring Lafayette suddenly received orders to join his regiment for summer maneuvers in the field. He spent no time with the King's Dragoons, however, going instead to Le Havre, where he lived incognito as a member of a small staff engaged in preparing a secret invasion of England.

In mid-June the invasion plans were abandoned and he was recalled to Paris. He spent ten days in the city. He stayed with Adrienne at the Hôtel de Noailles, and only members of the immediate family even knew he was in the city. He enjoyed no social life, paid no visits to Versailles, and saw neither Aglae nor his friends. Each morning he went to a small, inconspicuous house not far from Nôtre Dame, and there he spent the entire day conferring with two older men who reached the place separately. One was Benjamin Franklin, the other was the Comte de Vergennes, and together the three men made plans for a major French expedition to sail to America and take part in a campaign against the British.

The trust that both France and the United States placed in the twenty-two-year-old Gilbert de Lafayette was extraordinary. He was accepted as a military expert, and his advice was heeded. His sojourn in America had won him a high place in the councils of the mighty, even though he had won no battles of consequence or led more than three hundred men into a fight with the enemy.

More than his reputation as a hero was responsible. It was apparent that he knew what he was talking about, and his seriousness of purpose inspired confidence. Men of stature, French and American alike, recognized in him an ambitious kindred spirit.

Before going back to Le Havre, Lafayette purchased a portrait of General Washington and arranged to present it to the people of the United States at Dr. Franklin's house on Independence Day. When July 4 arrived, however, he was too busy to leave Le Havre, so Adrienne made the presentation on his behalf. The public duty was her first, and she handled herself well. Nineteen years old now, she appeared reconciled to the life of a hero's wife, a woman who had to endure long separations from him.

At the end of August Lafayette returned to Paris for a few days. He had grown tired of spending all his time in long planning sessions, and longing for action, he tried to persuade the Comte de Maurepas to give him a force of 2,000 men. He wanted young, agile troops, men who were familiar with infantry and artillery, men who were in sound physical condition. It was his intention to launch a series of raids against English coastal cities and towns; he argued that these attacks would disrupt the British, making it more difficult for them to wage war either in Europe or in the New World.

Few French senior commanders had ever fought in real battles, he declared, and his own experience made him the natural leader for such an expedition. Maurepas admired his stubborn tenacity, but vetoed the project, to his intense disappointment.

Lafayette's instincts were sound. In effect he was proposing the type of commando raids that the British utilized in World War II, tactics that kept the German armies occupying France off balance. He had been inspired by the principles used by American Indians in their assaults on frontier settlements, and had he been allowed to proceed, the military history of the next few years might have been far different. Lafayette was already proving he was an innovator, a man who refused to be bound by conventional ideas of warfare. Unfortunately, he was ahead of his time, and Maurepas lacked the imagination to match his daring.

Adrienne went to the country during the last weeks of her confinement, and settled into a family château at Passy. Two days before Christmas her husband came to Paris, intending to join her for the holidays. At 2:00 A.M. on Christmas Eve he was awakened by a courier bringing him a letter from Adrienne which informed him she had given birth to a son.

In his elation Lafayette, ignoring the hour, went to Dr. Franklin to tell him the baby would be named George Washington de Lafayette. On Christmas Day, after joining his wife, he wrote the news to General Washington, with whom he had been corresponding regularly.

A week later Lafayette returned to Paris for consultations with the Cabinet. It was becoming evident to him, as it was to other thinking men, that no military campaigns of consequence would develop in Europe for the simple reason that the French army was insufficiently organized for combat. The navy was strong and the country was wealthy, but the royal regiments, most of them commanded and staffed by amateurs, were incapable of waging war.

Tired of inactivity, writing reports, and making plans that failed to materialize, Lafayette began to think of returning to America. He conceived a two-pronged idea, one element of which was the acquisition of weapons and ammunition that could be turned over to General Washington. Maurepas and Vergennes agreed, and the ordnance department of the army soon collected 15,000 muskets, together with suitable supplies of bullets and gunpowder.

The second portion of Lafayette's plan required greater persuasion. He wanted France to send a corps of 10,000 to 15,000 troops to the New World to join the Americans. These men would be the elite of the French army, hand-picked from existing units. The corps, of course, would be commanded by Lafayette.

In principle the Cabinet approved of the scheme, but thought it too ambitious and whittled down the corps to 6,000 men. Ultimately a total of 4,000 actually made the voyage and fought at the side of the Continentals. Equally important, the realities of internal politics made it impossible to give the command to a man who held the rank of colonel in the French army. Experienced senior officers took precedence, and it was finally decided to award the post to the Comte de Rochambeau, an exceptionally competent veteran.

Demonstrating his firm understanding of military strategy, Lafayette insisted that the corps be accompanied by a fleet sufficiently powerful to break the British blockade of the American seaboard and keep open the lines of communication between the United States and France. Maurepas and Vergennes agreed.

Lafayette's own position was delicate. Common sense made it possible for him to swallow his disappointment, and he expressed a willingness to serve under Rochambeau, but indicated that he preferred to revert to his rank as a major general of the Continental Army. Neither the ministers nor the crown objected, and he was granted a leave of absence from the French army for the purpose.

In fact, the government went out of its way to accommodate him, and placed a forty-two-gun frigate, the *Hermione*, at his disposal for his return voyage to America. It was arranged that he would carry the weapons and munitions that would be turned over to General Washington.

His friends and relatives by marriage, Noailles and Ségur, immediately volunteered for duty under Rochambeau. Lafayette had made the American cause so popular that scores of other young nobleman also asked to join the expedition, giving Rochambeau his choice of officers.

On February 20, 1780, Major General Lafayette of the Continental Army went to Versailles in his blue-and-buff uniform to bid farewell to Louis XVI and Marie Antoinette. The King was amiable, as always, and the Queen went out of her way to express her confidence in Lafayette's future. She might dislike him, but she knew her duty sufficiently well to say the right thing at the right time.

Lafayette spent his final days with his wife and children in

Paris, and on March 4 he returned to Versailles for last-minute consultations with the Cabinet. He also picked up a number of letters for General Washington and the Congress. On the morning of March 6 he took his leave of Adrienne. Thereafter, until he boarded the *Hermione* on March 13, he wrote her at least one letter each day, sometimes two or three brief notes.

Bad weather delayed the departure of the frigate, which finally sailed on March 20. The voyage was uneventful, no British warships were encountered on the high seas, and on April 28 the *Hermione* reached Boston.

The city welcomed Lafayette with a joy that verged on hysteria. Cannon boomed, every church bell in the city pealed, and thousands came to the dock to welcome him. A huge throng escorted him to the legislature, where he listened to brief addresses and replied in kind. So many people wanted to shake his hand that the official reception was moved to the Common, where sides of beef were barbecued, and that night a huge bonfire was lighted, military bands played, and a fireworks display entertained the crowd.

The next morning Lafayette and his small personal staff left for New Jersey at the head of a wagon train carrying the weapons, ammunition, and gunpowder he was bringing to the Continentals. General Washington welcomed him as a son, and the staff received him as a comrade in arms. "I have come home," he wrote to Adrienne.

The military situation was anything but promising. The Continental Congress had printed so much paper money that its dollars were virtually worthless. The Continentals had been forged into a superior fighting force, but the militias of the various states, lacking food and uniforms, were unreliable, and when the commanders of regiments and battalions awakened in the morning they immediately asked how many men had deserted during the night.

Lafayette was too proud to tell the French government how precarious the American situation had become. Rather than lie, he wrote nothing.

In May the British captured Charleston, and a Redcoat force under General Lord Cornwallis was given the difficult task of subduing the Carolinas. General Sir Henry Clinton, the British commander, continued to occupy New York, where he made his headquarters.

On July 12 Rochambeau and his corps of 4,000 men arrived at Newport, escorted by a small squadron of warships. The principal French fleet, under the Comte de Grasse, had not yet sailed from Brest; although nobody in America yet knew it, it had been ordered, as its primary assignment, to protect the French-owned islands in the West Indies. A British fleet promptly blockaded Newport.

All French military and naval units that came to the United States were under direct orders from the crown to place themselves under the command of General Washington. Lafayette had insisted on this provision before he had returned to the New World in order to prevent confusion, but relations did not develop as he had anticipated.

The primary problem facing the Americans and the French was their inability to communicate with each other. Washington and his staff spoke no French, Rochambeau and his staff spoke no English. The Commander in Chief solved this problem, or so he thought, by assigning General Lafayette as his liaison officer.

Lafayette was enthusiastic and wanted action; Rochambeau was cautious and had no intention of risking disaster. Lafayette urged him to attack Sir Henry Clinton and take New York, but the commander of the French corps refrained. Almost inevita-

53

bly, friction developed between the brash young marquis and the careful veteran. Both remembered they were French nobles and remained polite, but first in Newport and later in Philadelphia their relations were strained. Certainly Rochambeau had no intention of taking orders from someone young enough to be his grandson, and Lafayette, trying to prod him into action, sometimes was inclined to forget it was his duty to relay Washington's requirements to the French, not give orders on his own authority.

Neither he nor Rochambeau wanted an open break, but both were frustrated and unhappy. The older man took a paternalistic approach, which caused the younger to feel he was being patronized. Washington, relying completely on Lafayette, seldom was even aware of the Gallic barbs that enlivened the intercourse of his liaison officer and the French high command.

Young officers like Noailles and Ségur, lacking Lafayette's genius and dedication, had the time of their lives. They were bored in conservative Newport, but Philadelphia entertained them extensively, and with nothing better to occupy their time they became involved in romances with local belles.

They failed to understand that the United States, under the influences of Puritans and Quakers, was not the court at Versailles. Lafayette knew the difference, however, and so severely lectured his relatives by marriage on the impropriety of engaging in romantic affairs that they sometimes called him "the bishop" behind his back and began to avoid him.

One duty performed by Lafayette during this period of relative inactivity once again brought him into the limelight. Major General Benedict Arnold, a brilliant but emotionally unstable officer who had been the real winner of the Battle of Saratoga, shocked his fellow Americans by defecting to the

British. His contact was Sir Henry Clinton's adjutant, Major John André, who made the fatal error of appearing behind American lines in civilian clothes. André, an exceptionally attractive and pleasant young man, was captured and necessarily placed on trial as a British spy.

Lafayette was appointed by Washington as a member of André's court-martial board. He and his colleagues had no real choice in reaching their verdict, all civilized countries accepting the convention that a military officer who appeared in enemy-occupied territory wearing civilian attire was a spy. André was found guilty and executed.

The British press mourned his death, which was natural, and of course emphasized the presence on the board of a French nobleman. That Americans should vote as they did was understandable; that a highborn Frenchman should be responsible for André's "murder" they found inexcusable. Utilizing the incident for propaganda purposes, the newspapers in London and the provinces launched savage attacks on Lafayette. The French press felt compelled to defend him, and he was so prominently featured in headlines that, in both France and England, the defection of Arnold was a secondary matter.

Early in 1781 a significant change took place in the military situation. Cornwallis, still trying in vain to bring the Carolinas under control, was dispatched to Virginia, where reinforcements were sent to him. Clinton had finally realized that Virginia, a primary source of American manpower, food, and other supplies, was the key to the war in the South. If Cornwallis could take Virginia, the Americans would collapse.

Washington was tied down in the North, and knew that if he left Clinton unattended the British would march from New York to Philadelphia. So he had to send someone he trusted to deal with Lord Cornwallis. His choice was Lafayette, who was given his first important command of 3,000 men.

For several months "the boy" and Cornwallis played a game of hide-and-seek. Lafayette, initially outnumbered two to one, maneuvered brilliantly as he avoided battle. Throughout the late winter and spring of 1781 he repeatedly proved that Washington's faith in him was justified. He was a natural commander of men, a superb tactician who instinctively avoided the traps the British set for him, yet he managed to keep the enemy off balance and made it impossible for Cornwallis to take Virginia. Somehow, during this difficult period, Lafayette also found ways to feed his troops and keep them clothed and supplied. No American commander had been more effective.

An augmented division under General Anthony Wayne was sent to help Lafayette, whose strength now equaled that of his foes. He took the offensive, and it was Cornwallis' turn to feint, duck, retreat, and evade. "The boy" was relentless in his pursuit, and his men, realizing they had the Redcoats on the run, gained confidence in themselves and in their commander.

Even before Lafayette was joined by Wayne, a grand strategic design was forming in his mind. Its execution would bring him lasting military renown and make him one of the true heroes of the American Revolution.

5

ALL THROUGH the spring of 1781 Sir Henry Clinton continued to send reinforcements to Virginia, until the forces serving under Lord Cornwallis outnumbered his own. Gradually the realization dawned on General Lafayette that George Washington was mistaken. The war would not necessarily be won or lost in the North, but could be won in Virginia.

The basic plan he evolved was simple. He proposed that Washington and Rochambeau march their respective armies to Virginia and join him for an all-out assault on Lord Cornwallis. A corps of reinforcements was already on the high seas, en route from France, and they, too, should come to Virginia.

The greatest danger was that the British, stronger at sea than the French, would blockade the Virginia coast. But Lafayette had a solution for this problem, too. A powerful French fleet under Admiral de Grasse, which included ships of the line and frigates as well as smaller warships, was already in the West Indies. He proposed that Admiral de Grasse sail north, neutralize the British fleet off the Virginia coast, and at the same time prevent Clinton from sending substantial reinforcements by sea to aid Cornwallis.

In letter after letter to the Commander in Chief Lafayette hammered at his theme. He wrote repeatedly to Admiral de Grasse, urging and cajoling, begging and nudging. He also wrote to Rochambeau again and again to win his support.

Ultimately Washington came to believe that Lafayette was right. In any event, the risk had to be taken. The military situation had deteriorated into a stalemate, and unless something decisive happened, the Americans, who had been struggling for independence since 1775, might well become discouraged. If the disciplined Continentals and veteran militiamen went home after their enlistments expired, the American cause was lost.

Admiral de Grasse reluctantly agreed to sail north for a limited period of time, but wrote that he could devote only a few weeks to a Virginia campaign. His primary assignment was the guarding of French interests in the Caribbean, and he would be in no position to fulfill his obligations if a stronger British fleet blew his warships out of the water.

In July Washington began to move his own troops and those of Rochambeau south, dispatching them in units no larger than battalions so that Sir Henry Clinton would not guess his intent.

Maintaining constant pressure on the British, fighting skirmishes when necessary but avoiding major battles, Lafayette compelled the Redcoats to retreat to Yorktown, at the mouth of the York River, to await evacuation by the Royal Navy. Cornwallis had boasted, "The boy shall not escape from me," but now the shoe was firmly on the other foot and it was the British who wanted to leave before they were overwhelmed.

Admiral de Grasse arrived before the Royal Navy could reach Yorktown, and Cornwallis was trapped. The Admiral was

nervous, however, and spoke daily of sailing back to the Caribbean. Lafayette had to use all his powers of persuasion, day
after day, to keep Admiral de Grasse on the scene. He was also
forced to tamp down the hotheads who wanted to attack the
British immediately.

Washington and Rochambeau arrived in September with a
joint force numbering between 6,000 and 8,000 men. Allied
pressure compelled Cornwallis to withdraw his entire force
toward Yorktown.

The "fifth act of the play," as Lafayette called it in a letter
to Maurepas, began on October 18, when Washington gave
the Marquis the honor of commanding the American center.
Lafayette's divisions attacked with verve and firm resolution,
and when they wavered their commander was in their midst,
sometimes urging them forward, sometimes setting the example by riding with the vanguard.

Cornwallis, badly outnumbered, was forced to surrender on
October 19. For all practical purposes his defeat signaled the
end of the British campaign in the United States. Clinton
continued ·to occupy New York until the peace treaty was
signed, two years later, and vicious battles remained to be
fought in the South, but the final outcome was no longer in
doubt. America had won her independence, and the hero of
Yorktown was General Lafayette.

On October 20 Lord Cornwallis entertained his young foe
at a private lunch, and the two men formed a friendship that
lasted for many years. The loser, a civilized man living in a
civilized era, even had the grace to apologize for the disparag-
ing personal remarks he had made about the winner. An
equally generous Lafayette accepted the apology.

In Richmond and Baltimore, Philadelphia and Boston and
other American cities, Lafayette was the hero of the hour, and

his popularity eclipsed even that of Washington. Ordinary citizens were overcome with wonder, and marveled that a foreigner with nothing personal to gain could have contributed so much to the cause of American liberty. Lafayette could do no wrong in the eyes of the American public, and everywhere he went he was mobbed by well-wishers. He was kept busy, he said, refusing the hundreds of gifts that people tried to give him.

Washington and his principal subordinates, among them Generals Greene, Knox, and Wayne, had even greater reason to be grateful to "the boy." They knew the worth of his contributions to their cause, and their affection for their unselfish French comrade-in-arms was deep. Every day at dinner they exchanged toasts with him, everyone involved vowing eternal friendship.

A French warship took the news of Yorktown to Europe in a month, and the press exploded. Paris newspapers called Lafayette "the savior of America," and the exaggerated cry was echoed throughout the Continent. Even the British press grudgingly admitted that the Marquis was a hero.

When Adrienne de Lafayette received a letter written by her husband on October 20, she, her mother, and her sisters went to church to offer their thanks to God.

Lafayette's mission in America was ended, and as soon as the dust of Yorktown settled he made plans to return home. *L'Alliance* again was made available to him, and he sailed from Boston on December 23, 1781, after a riotous farewell celebration in which virtually the entire city participated. Noailles, Ségur, and a few other gentlemen comprised his entourage.

Thanks to strong winds, *L'Alliance* dropped anchor at Lorient on the night of January 17. Lafayette was so anxious to reach home that he set out at once. He arrived late on the evening of January 21 and found the streets so crowded that it was difficult to ride through the throng. He learned that Paris was celebrating the birth of a dauphin, or crown prince, and that the entire nobility had gathered at the Hôtel de Ville to pay homage to the King and Queen. When he arrived at the Hôtel de Noailles he found only a few servants present, and had to be content to await his wife's return.

He had been recognized, however, and word soon reached the Hôtel de Ville that the hero had come back from the wars. Louis XVI immediately offered Adrienne de Lafayette the privilege of going home without delay, but she had been too well trained to depart while her rulers were still there.

Marie Antoinette graciously cut the ceremonies short and, in order to expedite Adrienne's homeward journey, gave her a place in the royal coach. Lafayette was astonished when the long procession of coaches, accompanied by the household cavalry, appeared in front of the Hôtel de Noailles.

He hurried outside and bowed to the Queen, offering his congratulations on the birth of her son. She returned the compliment by offering him felicitations on "the birth of America."

Adrienne was so excited that, when she saw her husband, she fainted in his arms. He carried her into the house, and the whole crowd applauded.

Lafayette was the man of the hour. Louis XVI granted him a special audience and, in the presence of the entire court, questioned him at length about Yorktown and the character of General Washington. At the climax of the audience Lafayette was presented with a commission as a major general in the French army; the honor of France was at stake, and the nation refused to be outdone by the United States.

A few days later the marshals of France held a dinner in

honor of the new major general, the guest list including every general officer in the army. Most of the brigadiers and major generals were in their forties and fifties, some of the marshals were in their seventies, and the guest of honor was twenty-four.

When Lafayette and his wife attended the opera the entire audience applauded him, and the prima donna escorted him to the stage, where he was crowned with a laurel wreath. Thanks to his exploits scores of young gentlemen applied for army commissions. Huge crowds gathered day and night outside the Hôtel de Noailles. The Cabinet, holding a special meeting in Lafayette's honor, offered him a scroll in which he was tendered the nation's thanks for his services. Rarely had any man of his age achieved such popularity.

Lafayette had to be careful in his public remarks. His sojourns in America had made him a convert to the democratic form of government, and France was still an old-fashioned monarchy in which all power emanated from the crown. The people had no voice in their government, and civil liberties were unknown. The young hero had picked up some dangerous ideas in the New World.

By spring Adrienne was pregnant again, to the surprise of no one. But her husband, who had been so straightlaced in America, was not devoting all of his time to her, and it was common gossip that he had renewed his casual affair with Aglae d'Hunolstein.

In the spring of 1782 Lafayette was presented to another lady, one who rarely went to court. Diane Adelaide de Damas d'Antigny was the wife of Charles François, Comte de Simiane and Marquis de Miremont, to whom she had been married for five years. They had no children. Lafayette may have met her through her brother, Charles de Damas, who had been one of his aides in America. Diane was a brunette, and her admirers said she was the most beautiful woman in France. It was said that she and her husband, who was reputedly effeminate, had a platonic relationship, but no scandal had ever touched her name. Her firm disapproval of the dissolute court kept her from Versailles.

Diane de Simiane apparently lost her heart to Lafayette when she first met him. He, as always susceptible to beauty, was unable to resist her, either, and it appears their affair was under way many weeks before he and Aglae d'Hunolstein decided to part company.

Everything that Lafayette said and did was news, so it is unlikely that Adrienne was unaware of his extracurricular activities. There was nothing she could do to halt his affairs, however, as they were sanctioned by custom, and it appears there was nothing she wanted to do. She was so much in love with him that she actually regarded herself as unworthy of him. It never occurred to her that she was her husband's real love, and that he indulged in his affairs only to amuse himself.

It is true that his relationship with Diane de Simiane deepened and lasted for many years, but she always took second place to his wife. Ultimately, after all of them had suffered great misfortunes during the French Revolution and its aftermath, the trio formed a curious relationship. Adrienne and Diane became close friends, and the Lafayette children referred to Diane as "aunt." The situation was not common but it was not unheard of either. It was expected that a man would have both a wife and a mistress; how charming it was, how much more pleasant for all of them, if they could be friends!

In September 1782 Adrienne gave premature birth to a daughter, and her husband named the girl Virginie, after his favorite American state. When Dr. Franklin heard the news he expressed the hope that the Lafayettes would remain sufficiently prolific to have twelve more children who could be named after the other American states.

That same month Lafayette celebrated his twenty-fifth birthday. Now he came into personal control of his fortune. He wanted a house of his own, and he instructed his financial agent to search for a suitable place. He also asked Adrienne to look for a house in town.

His own stay in Paris was cut short, France and Spain having decided to make war together against England. Admiral d'Estaing was given command of the joint naval operations, and Lafayette was appointed commander of the combined armies. Late in the autumn he and Estaing sailed together to Cadiz for conferences with Spanish generals and admirals.

These meetings soon degenerated into quarrels. Some of the participants wanted to attack Canada, while others preferred to make the British possessions in the Caribbean their target. Only Lafayette wanted to attack both.

King Charles III of Spain, whom Goya pictured as a simpleton in several famous portraits, proved he was wiser than most people believed. After one long meeting, during which Lafayette argued hard in favor of an attack on the island of Jamaica, the Spanish monarch observed privately to Admiral d'Estaing, "I'm against the plan. If Lafayette takes Jamaica he will turn it into a republic."

Private correspondence occupied a great deal of Lafayette's time after working hours. He wrote letters to Adrienne assuring her of his love and devotion. He wrote passionate letters to Aglae d'Hunolstein and somewhat more restrained love letters to Diane de Simiane. Nowhere in these communications did Lafayette repeat as much as a single phrase. His protestations of affection must be taken at face value, and it can only be assumed that each of the three ladies occupied a different niche. Certainly he was not unique in his approach; many other eighteenth-century gentlemen achieved similar precarious balances in their private lives.

The conferences with the Spaniards required many months of tedious negotiations, and Lafayette spent the better part of a year in Cadiz and Madrid. Late in August 1783 he and Estaing received word from Paris that the United States and Great Britain had concluded their negotiations successfully and that a peace treaty would be signed within a few days.

This development canceled the Franco-Spanish campaign, so the French officers returned to Paris, their long labors having been expended in vain. The Comte de Vergennes showed his gratitude for all that Lafayette had done by promoting him to the rank of marshal. He was awarded his baton, the symbol of his ultimate military authority, in a special parade-ground ceremony at Versailles. Anastasie and George Washington de Lafayette attended with their mother; it is the first known occasion that they made a public appearance.

Lafayette wrote to General Washington, congratulating him on the achievement of the peace treaty. He also outlined a plan he had been mulling over. He hated slavery, and he proposed that he and Washington buy some property together, purchase a number of slaves, set them free, and then pay them wages to work on the farm. Other Americans would be certain to follow Washington's example, he declared, and his own following in France and her territories was such that he believed he could guarantee the planters on the French islands in the Caribbean would follow suit, too.

This letter is the first in which Lafayette mentioned his opposition to slavery. Ultimately he would become Europe's most vocal champion of abolition and the granting of the franchise to blacks. Nothing in his background or training had prepared him for the stand he took on slavery, and subsequently on other issues. The inbred French aristocracy was reactionary and shortsighted, and Lafayette stood almost alone in his espousal of humane causes and civil liberties. He had first gone to America at an impressionable age, he had believed in the principles for which the Revolution had been fought, and with the lack of subterfuge that would mark his entire career he made his views plain. He had seen slavery at work in Virginia and it had disgusted him; he was opposed to it.

A number of personal problems occupied at least a part of his attention after his return to France. Not the least of them was the termination of his affair with Aglae d'Hunolstein, at her instigation. The court had been gossiping about her, the Duc de Chartres had threatened to break off with her, and she finally took matters into her own hands.

She notified Lafayette by letter that she would not see him again, and she kept her word, even though he made repeated efforts to get in touch with her. She also bade farewell to the Duc de Chartres, then retired to a country estate belonging to her husband. Even this withdrawal was not enough to satisfy her, and a few months later she entered a covent, where she remained for the rest of her life.

Lafayette did not remain in Paris for more than a short time. Adrienne had found a handsome house on the Rue de Bourbon, which he bought and furnished for a quarter of a million livres. While it was being put in order the couple paid several visits to his one surviving blood relative, his aunt Charlotte de Chavaniac.

He straightened out his aunt's tangled financial affairs and gave her a pension that would make her financially comfortable for the rest of her life. At considerable personal expense he made gifts of grain to his tenant farmers and officially forgave their debts to him, handsome gestures that increased his popularity. At Adrienne's suggestion he supplied the funds for the establishment of a factory that would make woolen cloth, and after she met with the priests of the area and learned their needs he contributed substantial sums to the local churches.

These gestures seem normal and natural to people of a later age, but they were almost without precedent in the late eighteenth century. Many French nobles drew revenues from their ancestral holdings throughout their entire lives without ever visiting their properties or showing any regard for the welfare of the peasants there. This selfish neglect caused a smoldering hostility that was one of the primary causes of the French Revolution, which would break out before the end of the decade. Adrienne saw to it that her husband continued to contribute to the people of Chavaniac, and it was this generosity that may have saved her from the guillotine when she was threatened at the height of the Revolution.

After the Marquis and Marquise returned to Paris, Lafayette was notified that he was being awarded the nation's highest decoration, the Cross of St. Louis. Ordinarily the honor was reserved for men of distinction who had served France for many decades, and never in the history of the order had the cross been given to someone so young. A ceremony was held in the king's chapel at Versailles, with only those who themselves held the Cross of St. Louis in attendance. The Duc d'Ayen, who presided, was proud to receive his son-in-law into the order.

The cross was one of two decorations that Lafayette wore for the rest of his life, although he was awarded many. The other was the Medal of Honor voted him by the Continental Congress on behalf of the people of the United States.

By the end of 1783 Lafayette's place in French society was

secure. His high birth and his wealth guaranteed him a niche at court, which he had chosen to reject, and it was his own exploits that had won him public esteem. He was a military and political adviser to the government, universally acknowledged as the primary liaison officer in dealings with the United States. Dozens of young officers clamored for the privilege of serving under him in the army. It was rumored that he would be appointed to a position in the government, and that at the very least he would be made minister to the United States.

He enjoyed such popularity, both in Paris and in his native Auvergne, that he could have demanded any position he wanted. But he had no political ambitions at this stage of his career. Americans continued to regard him as one of their own, and Dr. Franklin was a frequent visitor at the house on the Rue de Bourbon, as were John and Abigail Adams, among many others. A large portrait of George Washington greeted them in the drawing room, and swords presented to Lafayette by the Congress, the state of Virginia, the officers of the Continental Army, and the men of his own corps were on display in his library.

Late in 1783 and early in 1784 Lafayette became more deeply enmeshed in his affair with Diane de Simiane, and it was during this same period that Adrienne became friendly with her husband's mistress. Both were pious young ladies who devoted much of their time to helping the poor, neither was interested in the hedonistic luxury of Versailles, and they shared a high regard for the man they believed the greatest of the age. It did not occur to Diane, apparently, to attempt to wean Lafayette away from his wife and children, and a relieved Adrienne appeared willing to share him with her rival. Men whose domestic lives were far less tranquil than Lafayette's had good cause to envy him.

Still avoiding the frivolous court set, the Lafayettes began to move in what were regarded as the intellectual circles of Paris. The young marquis expressed himself freely at dinners and receptions, and his views gained wide circulation. He was loyal to the crown, but believed that too much power was concentrated in the monarchy. One of the first to recognize the smoldering discontent that soon would lead to the outbreak of the French Revolution, he advocated the granting of the franchise to all men who owned property, which included the nobility, many of the clergy, and—an innovation—the middle class, who presently enjoyed no privilege other than that of paying taxes. Even these modest reforms were thought of as radical by conservative nobles, who believed that Lafayette had been contaminated by the American experiment in government.

Always unorthodox, Lafayette unhesitatingly broke precedent. Late in 1783 an Englishman two years his junior, William Pitt the younger, second son of the Earl of Chatham and leader of the reform element in the House of Commons, paid a brief visit to Paris. He expressed a desire to meet Lafayette, and was immediately invited to the house on the Rue de Bourbon for dinner. Peace just having been restored, eyebrows were raised at Versailles.

Lafayette ignored his critics and invited Pitt to dine again the following day, at which time Dr. Franklin, John Jay, and other prominent Americans also were guests. It was necessary, Lafayette declared, for former enemies to talk, find a common meeting ground, and achieve an understanding. Men who discussed their problems across a dinner table were not likely to make war against each other.

Almost as soon as Pitt returned to London he was asked to form a new government, and became prime minister. Thereafter he was the leading force in British politics for many years, and for the rest of his life was on friendly terms with Lafayette, on one occasion remarking in Parliament that he admired him "as a liberal, as a statesman, as a patriot, and as a contributor to world order."

America continued to be foremost in Lafayette's thoughts, and in April 1784 he received a letter from George Washington that delighted him. The General had left public life, retiring as commander in chief of the Continentals, and had returned to the simple life of a planter at Mount Vernon, his Virginia estate. He invited Lafayette and Adrienne to visit him and Mrs. Washington there that summer.

Adrienne very much wanted to see her husband's beloved United States, but someone had to supervise his business affairs, a task she had long been attending. Besides, she could not bear the thought of being separated from her children for a period of several months, so she decided to remain at home.

Lafayette engaged a suite on a commercial packet boat and, accompanied by only one aide, left Lorient at the end of June. He arrived in New York a month later. It was the first time he had seen the place, which had been under British occupation during his earlier sojourns in America. The entire city turned out to greet him. The enthusiastic welcome was reminiscent of his arrival in Boston at the climax of the war.

An escort of militiamen and civilians accompanied him to Philadelphia. There he was invited to address the Congress, which had been reorganized under the Articles of Confederation, and the grateful people of the United States presented him with a tract of 10,000 acres in Virginia. In a speech of acceptance Lafayette indicated that nothing would please him more than to settle in the United States and make his permanent home there. It was a refrain he would repeat many times in the years ahead.

So many receptions were held in his honor in Pennsylvania, Delaware, and Maryland that they would have exhausted a man in less robust health. Eventually Lafayette reached Mount Vernon, and there he spent a "perfect fortnight."

Every morning he and his host went out for a canter. Each day they discussed the state of the world, the raising of crops, and the training of horses. Lafayette acquired a taste for fried chicken, and Mrs. Washington gave him a recipe to take home with him. In a letter to Adrienne he requested her to acquire a barometer and a copy of the Declaration of Independence for his library; he also suggested it might not be amiss if a rug were placed on the floor.

Only the presence of slaves on the estate marred the visit. Lafayette protested that they should be freed. Washington said the economy of the South would be ruined. It was their only disagreement.

Returning to Philadelphia, Lafayette was surprised when the tribes of the Iroquois Confederation, who were negotiating a new treaty with the United States, asked him to pay them a visit at their camp. He complied, and to the amazement of his escorts he was completely at home with the Indians, squatting before their fires, eating with his fingers, and sleeping in the open.

The Iroquois asked him to represent them in their dealings with the Congress. This he did, presenting their views with such clarity that both sides credited him with speeding the progress of the negotiations. Before leaving the Iroquois, Lafayette arranged to take a twelve-year-old boy of the Seneca tribe, named Kayenlaha, back to France with him. It was agreed that the boy would live with the Lafayettes for several years and be educated by them.

Several of the states conferred honorary citizenship for life on Lafayette, and before he left he was required to deliver another address to the Congress. He was given a standing ovation when he said, "May this great temple of liberty stand as a lesson to the oppressors, an example to the oppressed, a sanctuary for the rights of mankind."

Before embarking for home Lafayette paid another, brief visit to Mount Vernon to bid farewell to the man who called him his "adopted son." Washington gave him letters to take to every member of his family. Their parting was sad, Washington being convinced they would not meet again. Lafayette, however, expressed the certainty that he would return to America in the near future. He had no way of knowing that four tumultuous decades would pass before he would come to the United States again.

6

GILBERT AND Adrienne de Lafayette went to Versailles infrequently, but led an active social life in their house on the Rue de Bourbon. Every Monday was "American day," and regular dinner visitors included Dr. Franklin, John and Abigail Adams, and the recently arrived Thomas Jefferson, who formed a close friendship with the Marquis and whose concept of democracy profoundly influenced the family. Lafayette remained loyal to the crown, at least nominally, but he made no secret of his political leanings, and it was taken for granted at the court that he would welcome either the establishment of a republic or the promulgation of a constitution that would greatly diminish the power of the throne.

In some circles, including the Noailles-Ayen family, he was called the unofficial United States minister to France. Anastasie, who was seven years old, and George, who was five, had a special tutor who taught them English, and both children were always present on Mondays, when American guests came to the house. Kayenlaha, the Seneca, also was very much in evidence.

Lafayette continued to agitate for the abolition of slavery, and took it upon himself to initiate a specific campaign that would free all slaves in the French colonies in the West Indies. Various members of the Cabinet were personally sympathetic to the cause, but they did little or nothing officially, and in the spring of 1785 the Marquis decided to take matters into his own hands.

His first step was the purchase of two plantations in Cayenne for 125,000 livres, a price that included almost fifty slaves. It was his plan to grant them immediate emancipation, but the manager he hired to operate the plantations convinced him it would be wiser to work out a schedule of gradual emancipation. The blacks, who were illiterate, unskilled laborers, would be educated over a period of several years, and during that time they would be granted freedom on a step-by-step basis.

Never one to be concerned with day-to-day details, Lafayette was content to leave the supervision of the project to Adrienne, who shared his enthusiasm for emancipation. The project was largely ignored at the court, although the government was interested, and the Ministry of Colonies studied the reports that the Marquis submitted every few months.

Too restless to settle down into humdrum routine, Lafayette resumed his travels in July 1785, when he went off to the German states and Austria to learn what he could about their military establishments. The high point of his journey was a visit to Berlin, where he was received by the man generally recognized as the greatest soldier of the age, King Frederick II. They discussed military strategy by the hour, but Lafayette did not particularly enjoy the association. Frederick the Great was a tyrant, and had little in common with the twenty-eight-year-old French field marshal who had come to believe in liberty and equality for all people.

By happenstance Lord Cornwallis visited Berlin while Lafayette was there, and Frederick immediately saw to it that he
and Lafayette were seated next to each other at dinner. The
meal was a great success, the victor and loser of the Battle of
Yorktown spending several hours discussing every aspect of the
recent war in America.

Lafayette's stay in Vienna was somewhat shorter than he
had planned. The Austrian court was the most reactionary in
Europe, and the generals responsible for maintaining order in
a sprawling empire did not approve of the views so freely
expressed by the young Frenchman. He was graciously received
in both private and public audience by the Emperor Joseph II,
however, and Marie Antoinette's brother went out of his way
to express admiration for the exploits of the French hero.

After Lafayette's return to France he purchased another
property adjacent to Chavaniac out of the profits his estates
were earning. This acquisition made him one of the biggest
landowners in Auvergne, but he was not popular with his
aristocratic neighbors because he insisted on sharing his profits
with the peasants who worked for him. Some nobles began to
regard him as a dangerous visionary.

In the autumn of 1785 Lafayette was embarrassed when his
bust, done by the sculptor Jean Antoine Houdon, was presented to the city of Paris by the state of Virginia, which
specified that it should be placed on exhibit in the Hôtel de
Ville. There were many statues of great men in the old city
hall, but no man had ever before received such an honor in his
own lifetime. The government had no desire to offend France's
allies across the Atlantic, however, so it was decided to accede
to the request. Adrienne attended the unveiling ceremony,
accompanied by her children, but her husband was conspicuous by his absence. Even a man who loved applause apparently

found such an occasion too much to bear.

In his enthusiasm for all things American he worked closely with Jefferson in the expansion of Franco-American trade, and frequently went to the Cabinet with requests for new agreements. Late in 1785 he was responsible for the conclusion of a new treaty that trebled French imports of Virginia tobacco. Jefferson jokingly referred to him as "my principal assistant." In a letter to his close friend and colleague James Madison, Jefferson predicted that within a short time Lafayette would be given a high place in the government. Even while appreciating his many good qualities, Jefferson remarked that he had one weakness, an insatiable "appetite for popularity and fame, but he will get above this."

By 1786 France was beginning to disintegrate after more than a century of royal extravagance. Few men realized she was edging ever closer to open revolution, but the national treasury was empty, revenues were declining, and the country's debt was growing. It was obvious that something had to be done.

Lafayette saw an opportunity for major reform, and advocated the election of a congress by the people, in imitation of what the Americans had done. The crown and government were not prepared for such a drastic step, however, and instead Louis XVI appointed an "Assembly of Notables" to meet, assess the situation, and make recommendations. Lafayette was made a member over the objections of several Cabinet members who thought his views were too liberal.

Quarters were provided at Versailles for the Assembly, which met on a leisurely schedule in 1787. No one appears to have realized that the problems facing France were urgent, or that it was necessary to initiate changes immediately. The Assembly resembled a debating society that devoted its time and energies to the abstract discussion of philosophical issues.

In this hothouse atmosphere Lafayette gradually emerged as the articulate leader of the liberal faction.

He pressed for the abolition of slavery, calling the existence of the institution "a crime against Nature and man." He was equally firm in demanding the restoration of religious liberty to Protestants, their prerogatives having been denied since Louis XIV had revoked the Edict of Nantes, under which they had been granted freedom of worship by his grandfather, Henry IV. Thanks to his insistence Protestant children henceforth would be recognized as legitimate, Protestants were granted burial rights, and Protestants could enjoy the benefits of a legal marriage—provided a couple could find a minister who would perform the marriage ceremony.

In a display of courage much admired by his friends, Lafayette also attacked the corruption that reached into the highest places. Greedy men who held posts of public trust, he charged, were pocketing funds intended for public purposes, and were becoming wealthy at the expense of the people. Government bureaucrats did not appreciate his blunt candor.

In mid-March of 1787 Lafayette took to bed with what a later age would call bronchitis. His ailment served as a convenient excuse for him to withdraw temporarily from the limelight. The Comte de Simiane, despondent because he had become impotent and suffering because of his wife's continued infatuation with the Marquis, had put a pistol to his head and killed himself.

News of the scandal spread swiftly. Anonymous conservatives, anxious to discredit Lafayette, financed the publication of a pamphlet that described his affair with Diane de Simiane in lurid terms and included a pathetic suicide note purportedly written by her husband. Street entertainers began to sing scurrilous ballads about Lafayette and the lady, too, but he was still popular with the general public, and the singers soon changed their tune. Lafayette rode out the storm in silence, hibernating at home.

When he returned to the Assembly of Notables in May 1787, he soon demonstrated that he had not lost his voice. Other thinking men were sharing his feeling of restlessness, but he was the first to demand that King Louis not only revive the States-General but convoke a national assembly for the purpose of transforming the many recommendations of the Assembly of Notables into law. The time had come when it was necessary to prepare a written constitution that would give the people a voice in the nation's government. Stability was essential, and France was in a state of increasing chaos. Inflation was rampant, the price of bread was doubling every month, and he predicted that the people would erect barricades in the streets unless something drastic was done.

His stand did nothing to increase Lafayette's popularity at court, where Marie Antoinette openly called him "a traitor to his class."

The government continued to move at the pace of the proverbial snail, and not until 1788 were provincial assemblies convened throughout France. Lafayette, of course, was a delegate to the Assembly of Auvergne, which met at Clermont-Ferrand, and there he expressed his views with such vigor that the Vicomte de Beaune, who presided, rebuked him for "espousing republican principles." Other conservatives attacked him for trying to win the support of poor members of the nobility and of the middle class.

The immediate result of his efforts was greater popularity throughout Auvergne. Late in 1787 he had been appointed to the important post of inspector general of the army, and he was believed to have won the support of his military colleagues, particularly the younger officers, who idolized him. He appeared to be in a strong position to make his views heard.

Lafayette's actual position at this time was anything but radical. In spite of the alarms of the court and the more conservative members of the Cabinet, he was a gradualist who had no desire to abolish the monarchy, only to reform it. Now thirty-one years of age, he recognized abuses and wanted to correct them before the advocates of more violent methods caused a far more drastic deterioration of the status quo. His approach, idealistic and somewhat naive, was best expressed in a letter he wrote to a friend, in which he explained his goals:

> A sufficient degree of fermentation to produce a threat of civil war, though without letting it materialize; in the army, enough of patriotism to worry the government, without causing actual disobedience; in the collection of taxes, a sufficient number of obstacles to lead to capitulation, though not to bankruptcy. The general effect of all this will lead us, by the shortest possible road, to the winning of that constitutional liberty for the attainment of which other countries have not thought torrents of blood and a hundred years of wars and misfortunes too high a price to pay.

His own words reveal a lack of political acumen, but he convinced himself that his approach was right, and his French friends lacked the political sophistication to tell him that no one could walk the tightrope he had stretched above the abyss. Jefferson and others who knew better kept their own counsel, realizing that when Gilbert de Lafayette had plotted his course he could not be persuaded to change it.

He himself brought matters to a head when twelve members of the Breton Assembly who demanded action in strident terms were imprisoned in the Bastille for their impertinence.

Lafayette was outraged, and reacted by writing a letter of protest to the Cabinet, denouncing the government in the Auvergne Assembly, and then writing an angry letter to King Louis. When Marie Antoinette wanted to know why he was concerning himself with affairs in Brittany, he sent her a reply that reflected his exasperation: "My relations with Brittany are the same as the Queen's with Austria."

According to the narrow-minded standards that had prevailed in France for centuries, Field Marshal the Marquis de Lafayette was guilty of treason. But he was still so popular that neither Louis XVI nor the Cabinet had the temerity to order his arrest. Instead they chose lesser forms of punishment: He was dismissed from his post as inspector general of the army, and was informed that his presence was no longer desired at court.

The dismissal of the hero was instrumental in polarizing popular opinion, and the house on the Rue de Bourbon overnight became a gathering place for intellectuals, dissidents, and reformers. According to one of the ministers it was "a hotbed of Americans and other republicans."

The government was bankrupt, but refused to admit it. Marie Antoinette was hissed when she rode in her carriage through the streets of Paris, and thousands of hitherto loyal citizens refrained from doffing their hats when they saw King Louis.

The government responded to the crisis by summoning the Assembly of Notables back into session. Lafayette became a member of a group known as the Thirty, all of them convinced that only the establishment of a constitutional monarchy would save France. He became intimate with other members of the group whose names would loom large in the history of the period, among them the Duc de Rochefoucauld, who shared his liberal philosophy. Another was the Abbé Sieyès, who became one of the principal philosophers of the French Revolution and later played a major role in the events that led to the rise of Napoleon Bonaparte. Yet another was the astonishingly crafty Charles Maurice de Talleyrand-Périgord, a churchman who was excommunicated by the Pope for, among other things, recommending the confiscation of church property to raise funds for government operations. He survived the Revolution, and, after serving as Napoleon's foreign minister, held the same post under the Bourbons after the Restoration. As members of the Thirty who believed that only the creation of a constitutional monarchy would save France, these men looked to Lafayette as their spokesman.

The country continued to crumble, becoming increasingly ungovernable, and late in 1788 the crown and Cabinet at last succumbed to pressure and called a meeting of the States-General for the following spring.

Lafayette became a candidate from Auvergne, and in March 1789 he went to Chavaniac to win the support of his fellow nobles in the district. He took with him a declaration of rights that he had written, a document remarkably similar to the American Bill of Rights, the first ten amendments to the Constitution, which would be adopted that same year. Many of his fellow aristocrats regarded these guarantees of personal liberty as violently radical, and he won election to the States-General by a narrow margin, only his record as a hero preventing him from suffering a defeat.

When he returned to Paris in April he learned from his wife that he was in danger of being arrested as a rebel. His popularity was one of the factors that saved him from imprisonment. Another was the rapid disintegration of civil order. Mobs roamed the streets of Paris, citizens who looked prosperous were robbed and beaten, and the homes of known supporters of the crown were sacked. Revolution was in the air.

The States-General convened on May 5, and Lafayette was a center of attention, supported by Noailles, Ségur, and others known as "the Americans," as well as by such liberals as Rochefoucauld.

Problems of organization occupied the States-General during its first weeks, and when it became so unruly that Louis XVI ordered it to disband, the delegates ignored the order. Prominent among those who defied the crown was Lafayette. Bound by his promises to his electors, he could not openly espouse the movement to convert the States-General into a national constituent assembly, but when the movement succeeded he was among those who rejoiced.

The process of disintegration continued. French troops no longer being regarded by the government as reliable, several regiments of German and Swiss mercenaries were hired to guard Louis and Marie Antoinette. On July 8 Lafayette made a speech in the National Assembly in which he demanded, in his usual blunt manner, that the "foreign troops" leave French soil without delay.

Seventy-two hours later he presented his Declaration of the Rights of Man and of Citizens to the Assembly, a move that convinced the court he wanted to set up a republic. This was not the case, but even his friends thought he had deserted the crown.

On July 13 Lafayette achieved even greater prominence. The aged archbishop of Vienne was president of the Assembly, and when it became apparent that the body would hold an all-night meeting, it was equally obvious that the elderly clergyman lacked the physical stamina to act as chairman. Lafayette was nominated and elected vice-president, and after the night-long session it was he who officially received word, on July 14, that a mob of Parisians had attacked the Bastille.

He raced into the city, hoping to calm the disorders, and made a pacifying speech to a crowd of thousands. At its conclusion he was elected by acclamation as head of the Paris militia, a body of citizen-soldiers that took the name of the National Guard.

Refusing to accept a salary, Lafayette struggled valiantly to prevent mob rule in a city gone berserk. Only his presence restored order, and for twenty hours out of each twenty-four he hurried from one trouble spot to another. Displaying his customary physical and moral courage, he defied hostile mobs, used persuasion when possible, and threatened firmness when necessary. Gouverneur Morris, soon to become American minister to France, wrote that only Lafayette's commanding presence prevented Paris from being destroyed.

On July 17 King Louis came to Paris, and Lafayette, commanding a mammoth force of 200,000 men, personally rode beside the royal carriage to protect the monarch. At the Hôtel de Ville someone handed Louis the red-and-blue cockade of the city of Paris, demanding that he wear it, and the frightened monarch placed the colors in his hat adjacent to the white cockade of the Bourbons.

Lafayette, seeking a reconciliation and seeing an opportunity, declared that red, white, and blue were the colors of the "new France," so it was he who inspired the establishment of the cockade that became the official emblem of the Revolution and whose colors have been retained in the French flag down to the present day.

Never had General de Lafayette achieved such popularity. People of all classes regarded him as the savior of the country, and Morris wrote that he had become "the unofficial king of

Paris and, perhaps, of the whole of France."

Inadvertently, too, he became the symbol of a savior. His vanity led him to ride a white horse, making him instantly recognizable wherever he went. His approach when danger threatened gave rise to the cry that "the man on horseback" or "the man on the white horse" had arrived. Lafayette became synonymous with authority; not until a century later did the phrase "man on horseback" assume a more sinister meaning.

Anarchy threatened on every hand, leading conservatives were being hanged by unruly mobs, and the National Assembly, spellbound by its own rhetoric in Versailles, was powerless. King Louis's brothers decided that discretion was the better part of valor, and fled from the country with their families.

The fires of revolt were breaking out faster than Lafayette could extinguish them. Totally exhausted after less than ten hours of rest in a week, he resigned as commander of the National Guard on July 22 and went home to sleep.

A few hours later a delegation representing every body of political opinion called on him and begged him to reconsider. They told him that only he, the Hero of Two Worlds, could save France. Unable to resist the flattery and taking the delegation at its word, he withdrew his resignation, mounted his white horse again, and returned to his impossible task. Only his presence prevented a collapse of the entire nation into anarchy.

He was too busy to attend the meetings of the National Assembly at Versailles, but he managed to keep in touch with proceedings there. On August 4 the Vicomte de Noailles, his good friend and brother-in-law, presented a motion that would voluntarily strip the nobility of its many privileges. Without hesitation Lafayette sent Noailles his proxy vote in favor of the resolution, even though it meant the loss of a major part of his great fortune.

Lafayette was making no mere gesture, and was sincere in taking this stand. That same day he found the time to write a brief note to Diane de Simiane, who had retired to her country estate far from the turmoil of Paris, and told her that "liberty for all is worth any sacrifice." Perpetually optimistic, he clung to the belief that out of the chaos a truly representative government of the people, modeled on the American system, would emerge.

Few men agreed with him, and among the most dubious were members of the American community in Paris. They realized that tensions were still mounting, and that only Lafayette, acceptable to those of almost every political persuasion, was preventing the outbreak of a vicious civil war. They marveled at his self-confidence and feared the worst.

7

THROUGHOUT THE SUMMER and early autumn of 1789 France inched closer to the abyss. Louis XVI would not reign, his Cabinet could not govern, and the National Assembly endlessly debated theoretical questions, chief among them being the kind of government that should be established in France. The only authority in the country was Lafayette, supported by the National Guard.

Money in the capital was so scarce that it became impossible for suppliers to purchase wheat from the farmers in the provinces, and by the beginning of October there was a severe shortage of bread in Paris. The mobs became ugly, and on October 5 a huge crowd formed at the Hôtel de Ville, intending to march to Versailles and storm the palace.

Lafayette, afraid that the appearance of his troops would start a riot in which many people would perish, rode alone to quiet the crowd. He was threatened with pikes, pistols, axes, and the gibbet by the infuriated, hungry citizens, but his calm was astonishing, his courage remarkable. His conduct awed the mob, and he was unmolested, but the people were beyond reason, and ultimately he withdrew.

The time had come to protect the royal family, and he made a forced march to Versailles at the head of five battalions of the National Guard. Outside the palace he halted his troops and required them to renew their oath of allegiance to the crown.

The small body of household troops was afraid to admit his battalions, so Lafayette said he wanted to enter the grounds alone. He stalked into the audience chamber, where a large group of nobles was convened. He knew everyone present, and either by blood or marriage was related to many.

A silence fell as he walked to the throne, removed his hat, and bowed to King Louis.

"Here is Cromwell," someone remarked.

Lafayette's scornful reply became one of his most famous remarks. "Monsieur," he said, "Cromwell would not have come here alone."

Most members of the court regarded him as the archtraitor. They were incapable of realizing that in favoring a constitutional monarchy he was not being personally disloyal to the crown. Lafayette would have preferred a republican form of government if it could have been established without wholesale revolution, but he knew it could not. A constitutional monarchy seemed the best solution under the circumstances. But a constitution granting any power, however limited, to the people would necessarily circumscribe the power of the crown. Advocacy of any diminution of royal power was treason in the eyes of the court. The aristocrats were capable of seeing the situation only in blacks and whites.

Their hostility complicated Lafayette's task of trying to arrange for the safety of the royal family. Shortly after midnight, his task not yet completed, he was informed that a mob had broken into the barracks of the National Guard. He rode there immediately, somehow persuaded the mob to withdraw, and restored order. Then, totally exhausted, he went to the nearby Hôtel de Noailles for a few hours of sleep.

Before dawn he was awakened by a sentry who told him a mob had broken into the palace. He rode there at once and, maneuvering his National Guard troops with skill and patience, obtained a disengagement. Several members of the household staff had been killed, and the mob had actually reached the entrance to Marie Antoinette's private apartment when Lafayette arrived. He used no actual physical force, but was able to insinuate his troops between the door and the crowd, and that broke the spell.

A frightened king and queen appeared on a balcony, and a huge crowd that had broken into the grounds stood below, jeering and threatening the lives of the royal couple. Louis promised to move into Paris immediately, but even this did not placate the people.

Suddenly Lafayette appeared on the balcony in his National Guard uniform. He stood at attention and saluted Louis, then bent low to kiss Marie Antoinette's hand. The mood of the mob changed, thanks to his deliberate dramatic gestures, and the King and Queen were cheered. Perhaps it was Lafayette who was being applauded. No one knew for certain, but even the members of the court who hated him had to admit he had saved the lives of the royal pair.

Early that afternoon a long procession moved into Paris. A battalion of the National Guard formed the vanguard, others taking up strategic places in the line. Louis and Marie Antoinette rode together, and scores of other carriages were filled with members of the court and deputies who had been attending the meetings of the National Assembly. A crowd of twenty or thirty thousand accompanied the procession, and by the time it reached the Hôtel de Ville it had grown to a quarter of a million.

Lafayette rode his white horse close to the open window on King Louis's side of the royal carriage, his drawn sword in his hand. His deliberate symbolism was not lost on the marchers or the hundreds of thousands who watched the parade through the streets of Paris. It was the duty of the National Guard to maintain order, and its commander intended to kill any man who dared to attack the King. The people respected Lafayette's courage, but that ride marked the beginning of a decline in his popularity. The citizens of Paris, like the aristocrats, saw the situation only in blacks and whites, and branded Lafayette as a royalist.

He escorted the royal family to the Tuileries, where the committee ruling the city decreed they should live, even though the place had been unoccupied for many years. Marie Antoinette is said to have remarked to him that she was sure she would never leave the place alive.

Lafayette posted reliable troops around the palace, arranged for their relief early in the morning, and, scarcely able to sit in his saddle, went home at 2:00 A.M. Before staggering off to bed he learned that a relieved and dutiful Adrienne had already written the news of his latest exploits to Diane de Simiane.

All through the autumn of 1789 and the winter months that followed, Lafayette appeared to be the only man in France capable of keeping the peace. He was the commander of the National Guard, charged with maintaining order and protecting the person of the King. He was the acknowledged leader of the largest political group in the National Assembly, the moderate reformers who wanted a constitutional monarchy. In the absence of an effective government he performed many of the functions of the various ministers, and he handled major matters relating to foreign affairs, finance, and security.

Gouverneur Morris sensibly told him he was accepting too great a burden, that no one man could govern the nation alone. The weary and harassed Lafayette shrugged and replied, "I would be grateful for help, but I am given none."

He conferred almost daily with King Louis; he attended debates at the Assembly, where the impending bankruptcy of the country was the principal topic of discussion; and he received visitors by the score in his drawing room. Mme Germaine Necker de Staël, daughter of the former finance minister, a woman endowed with an extraordinary intellect, became his close adviser during this period, and after the crowds left the house on the Rue de Bourbon late at night, she stayed behind to talk with him and with Adrienne. She, too, urged him to find others who would help, but men were reluctant to accept responsibilities in such a chaotic time.

Some of the tasks he was required to perform were embarrassing. The Duc d'Orléans, Louis's cousin, who had been Lafayette's rival for the hand of Aglae d'Hunolstein, was suspected—with justice—of conniving to win the throne for himself. Any such threat was an invitation to complete disorder, and Lafayette was obliged to send Orléans into exile in England.

A number of the Marquis's friends repeatedly urged him to take a new title, that of general in chief, and to assume all powers himself and clean house. His sense of legitimacy was so strong, however, that he refused these suggestions. Ultimately, he insisted, the situation would become stable again, and he prodded the National Assembly to form a constitution on the American model. His love of the American system blinded him; what he failed to recognize was that the people of France, unlike the people of the United States, wanted no such system. It is obvious that he lost sight of the first principle of a democracy, that a nation is governed with the consent of its citizens.

Lafayette toiled unceasingly through the early months of 1790, seeking no honors or permanent position for himself. If he envisaged himself as prime minister in a constitutional monarchy, which some of his supporters favored, there is no record in his correspondence of reported conversations that he sought such a post. At the same time he appears to have been blind to the gathering strength of the forces that were on the verge of sweeping away the entire monarchical apparatus. He remained so enamored of the American system that he was convinced his compatriots would adopt it when they understood it.

That faith, unsupported by fact, may have been his greatest weakness. Another was his continuing love of applause. He held real power, he was the symbol of power, and sycophants were able to gain his ear by flattering him. Speeches praising his wisdom and strength were made almost daily in the National Assembly, and he was still cheered as he rode through the streets of Paris, although the roars of approval were less vociferous than they had been.

Plans were made to create an amphitheater in the Champ de Mars and to hold ceremonies there before an "altar of the nation" on the anniversary of the seizure of the Bastille. Long rows of seats would be carved out of the ground, and Lafayette was asked to dig up the first spadeful of earth. He not only complied, but spent an entire morning at work with the spade.

The acid-tongued Marie Antoinette accurately mirrored the reactions of the royal family and the court to the ascension of the Marquis to power. "I truly believe," she said, "that Monsieur de Lafayette wants to save us. But who will save us from Monsieur de Lafayette?"

If Lafayette refused to see what was in store for France, others were more sensitive to the trends of the times. The Duc d'Ayen quietly departed from France and bought a château in Switzerland, where he lived with his current mistress. A number of Adrienne's other relatives left Paris for their country estates, and some of them followed the example of the King's brothers and went into voluntary exile. The signs were not difficult to read, and one of the clearest was the confiscation of church property, which made the nation temporarily solvent. Bishops were "elected," a move that caused a direct conflict with the Pope, and the salaries of the clergy were paid by the government.

The devout Adrienne de Lafayette was badly upset by these developments. Her husband, who was not a practicing Catholic but had respect for all religions, was distressed. He could do nothing to further his conviction that all men should be free to worship as they pleased, however, as any such stand would have brought him into direct conflict with the majority in the National Assembly, and he would have been dismissed from the position that was the key to his power, the command of the National Guard. His position grew increasingly precarious.

People of all political persuasions knew that France was in a state of transition, no one could predict in which direction the nation would head, and the man responsible for keeping the peace and maintaining a precarious balance gradually became the target of all elements.

The nobles continued to regard Lafayette as a traitor, and no one vilified him more consistently than the Marquis de Mirabeau, his principal rival for power. A society of radicals, who called themselves the Jacobins, were determined to destroy the monarchy, and knew that in the process they had to bring down Lafayette, too. So they spread a story, totally false, to the effect that he was Marie Antoinette's lover.

On April 18, 1791, Louis XVI precipitated a crisis by refusing to take communion from a priest in the pay of the National Assembly and insisting he wanted to go to Saint-Cloud, where he could receive communion from a priest of his own choice. Lafayette, true to his own principles, supported his decision and promised him safe-conduct. The Assembly protested, and a huge crowd of angry citizens gathered outside the Tuileries. The frightened king changed his mind.

Lafayette, believing his own authority had been questioned, promptly resigned as head of the National Guard.

No one was prepared to take his place, and even his enemies were horrified. Callers of every political persuasion went to the house on the Rue de Bourbon and attempted to persuade him to change his mind, but he refused. He was loyal to the country, its laws, and the crown, he said, and he could not be placed in a position of conflict between the people and the King.

No one of stature seemed willing or able to replace Lafayette, and the crisis grew worse. For eight days he refused to budge, but on April 26 he was presented with petitions from the officers and men of fifty-seven out of the sixty battalions of the National Guard, begging him to reconsider. He wavered, then rescinded his resignation.

This reversal may have been the worst error in judgment he ever made. He resumed his command of the Guard, and on the surface the balance was restored. By giving in, however, he destroyed the moderates' confidence in him, and he gave the radicals a chance to redouble their attacks on him. Now they called him a sly conniver who had deliberately created a crisis in order to enhance his own standing. Lafayette did not yet realize it, but he had made his position untenable.

In spite of the growing turmoil, Lafayette clung to his stubborn belief that the country was drawing closer to the establishment of a constitutional monarchy. The royal family did not share that view any more than did the National Assembly, and late in the spring, when the King privately received word that fifteen regiments loyal to him were mustering in the south, he began to make plans to escape from Paris.

His plans could not be kept completely secret, and rumors soon reached Lafayette, who had taken full responsibility for keeping the royal family at the Tuileries. He took the precaution of increasing the size of the National Guard units on duty at the palace.

On the night of June 20, 1791, Louis and Marie Antoinette made good their escape.

Lafayette heard the news early the following morning, and immediately sent parties of cavalrymen in pursuit, ordering them to bring back the King and Queen, unharmed. His own position was difficult; the radicals promptly charged him with connivance in the plot, and demanded his summary execution.

Displaying his customary courage, Lafayette went alone to the National Assembly. There he announced that the King and Queen had succeeded in escaping, and he outlined the steps he had taken to retrieve them.

One of his patrols captured Louis and Marie Antoinette, and on June 25 they were returned to Paris. Demonstrations for and against them were forbidden, and National Guard troops lined the route they took to the Tuileries. Lafayette's position was painful in the extreme: It was his duty and his wish to protect the persons of the King and Queen, and at the same time he was required to carry out the will of the National Assembly. Given his own choice, as he told Louis XVI in so many words, he would have favored the establishment of a republic, but his honor compelled him to play a contradictory role. He carried out the assignment with great dignity.

But the ill-considered, unsuccessful flight of the King made it impossible for the moderates to prevail, and Lafayette was caught in the middle. The aristocrats and conservatives hated him because he had recaptured the King. The radicals loathed him because they believed he had been a party to the escape. The ranks of men of goodwill were shrinking, ordinary citizens in the provinces as well as in Paris were taking the law into their own hands, and foreign diplomats regarded it as increasingly unlikely that France could solve her political problems peacefully.

On July 14, 1791, the second anniversary of the fall of the Bastille, a huge mob rioted on the Champ de Mars. Several battalions of the National Guard were called out to restore order, and Lafayette, who could have placed a subordinate in charge, took personal command of the troops.

The rioters shouted that they wanted his head, and when they tried to attack him the troops fired. A number of people were killed, and the word swept through Paris that Lafayette, the puppet of the King, had finally shown his true colors. There could be no doubt that Lafayette's days as head of the Guard were numbered. The fact that he had been forced to order his troops to fire on fellow Frenchmen disturbed him, and he told his wife he would leave the Guard at the first opportunity.

On September 4 the National Assembly finished its task of drawing up a constitution, and Louis XVI formally accepted the document. In theory, at least, a constitutional monarchy now prevailed.

Lafayette felt that his work was done. Ever mindful of the example set by his friend and personal hero, George Washington, he resigned from the National Guard and expressed his intention of living in quiet retirement on his estate in Auvergne. Whether he would have accepted a high post in the new regime had it been offered to him is open to question.

Honors were heaped on him in a farewell ceremony; the National Guard presented him with a handsome sword and the troops paraded before him. On September 20 he and his family left Paris, his son riding with him in one carriage while his daughters accompanied Adrienne in another. Auvergne gave him a riotous welcome, and he was still the Hero of Two Worlds. His letters to Diane de Simiane and to Washington, now the president of the United States, indicate he believed France had overcome her problems, and he was satisfied, almost smug, in his conviction that he had played a major role in the introduction of a new, peaceful era.

He left behind him a legacy of hatred. The radicals, still intent on destroying the monarchy, placed him high on their list for future execution. Marie Antoinette indicated to her few remaining intimates that life was more tolerable now only because she would not be obliged to see Lafayette again and to treat him with civility.

Lafayette was aware of none of this. His aunt, Charlotte de Chavaniac, was delighted to see him and his family, and he settled into his château with enthusiasm. Again following the lead of Washington, he imported English cattle, sheep, and pigs to improve his breeds, and he introduced American corn to his farms, obtaining seeds through the kindness of Jefferson. He also planned to grow tobacco, although he was inclined to believe the climate might be too cold.

His expenses during the American Revolution and the current inflation in France had eaten away about half of his fortune, but Lafayette was never one to worry about money. He ate into his capital in order to make major improvements in the château, and he appeared to have no worries as he took up the life of a country gentleman. Adrienne, as always, had to wrestle with the day-to-day problems of curbing her husband's extravagances and making ends meet. Lafayette himself refused to concern himself with such things. He had been wealthy since childhood, and at the age of thirty-four it did not occur to him that there might be a limit to what he could spend.

His stay at Chavaniac was brief. By December it was becoming apparent that the enemies of France, encouraged by her noble refugees, were planning to go to war to prevent the spread of revolutionary ideas. "The French ailment," said a wag in the British House of Lords, using a phrase that for centuries had meant venereal disease, "has become virulent, and its spread must be prevented."

The new French government, insecure and timid, realized that something had to be done, and 75,000 men were called to the colors for duty in the north and northeast. They would be divided into three armies, each composed of approximately 25,000 troops, and their mere appearance in the field, it was reasoned, would cool the martial ardor of France's potential foes. Each army would be placed under the command of a marshal, and the three nominated were the Comte de Rochambeau, Nicolas Luckner, and the Marquis de Lafayette— "Americans" all.

Louis XVI was for all practical purposes the prisoner of his subjects in the Tuileries, but he still wore a crown and the nominations were submitted to him. He balked when he saw the name of Lafayette and refused to sign the commission. The members of the new cabinet had to explain the situation to him in simple terms: If the Hero of Two Worlds was excluded, officers and enlisted men alike would refuse to serve, and the entire effort would be stillborn. The King signed.

The Ministry of War sent Lafayette notification of his appointment, and he received the communication on December 20. At long last he had the opportunity to lead a major French force against foreign foes, and the smell of gunpowder drove everything else from his mind. Glory beckoned, and neither his plans for Chavaniac nor the approach of Christmas could detain him. In spite of Adrienne's acute distress, punctuated by the first protests she had ever uttered, he left home the following day and arrived in Paris on Christmas Eve.

He was told he would make his headquarters at Metz, where he had last served as a junior officer. He was so eager to reach his post that, after paying token visits that evening to those of his wife's relatives who were still in the city, he spent Christmas Day on the road. His pace was so rapid that he exhausted his aides.

Lafayette had his hands full at Metz. Aristocratic officers had vanished from their posts and become refugees, daily fights broke out between conscripts and volunteers, and morale did not exist. Reminded of the chaos he had known during his first tour of duty in the American War of Independence, Lafayette acted accordingly, tightening the reins and instituting firm discipline.

The government in Paris neither helped him nor supported his efforts. His letters to Adrienne reflected his disgust with the "Jacobin rabble," represented by such leaders as Georges Jacques Danton, Maximilien Robespierre, and Camille Desmoulins, and he realized they were gaining the upper hand over men who were friendly to him, like the Abbé Sieyès and the Marquis de Condorcet. The radicals knew the outbreak of war was inevitable, and encouraged it, but did nothing to prepare for it.

In a remarkable letter to Adrienne, written from Metz on April 18, 1792, Lafayette summarized his own unenviable but firm position:

> . . . as I have already made clear, the French nation is my only party, and my friends and I are at the disposal of anyone who will act for the best, defend liberty and equality, uphold the Constitution, and reject everything that might tend to give it either an aristocratic or republican coloring. When the will of the nation, expressed by the elected representatives of the people and by the King, shall have declared that war is inevitable, I shall do everything in my power to bring it to a successful conclusion.

A man who wrote in such resounding terms to his wife might be suspected of creating a record for the sake of posterity, but this does not seem to be the case. Scores of the letters he sent to Adrienne and to Diane de Simiane are filled with his high-flown rhetoric and unselfish, patriotic resolve. He used such language because that was the way he actually thought. Those experienced in politics who claimed he was too naive for his own good or that of France were accurate in their appraisals.

Late in the spring the government ordered an attack on the enemy forces gathering in Belgium. Lafayette's regiments were not involved, and his colleagues failed to distinguish themselves. The Austrian regiments they opposed sent them into headlong flight to the Citadel at Lille. The shocked citizens of Paris lost their heads, and on June 20, 1792, a howling mob, blaming Louis XVI for the battlefield misfortunes, broke into the Tuileries and threatened the King.

This indignity, as unjust as it was senseless, infuriated Lafayette, who went without delay to Paris. There he went to the Assembly with a straightforward proposal: He would review the

National Guard, then lead it against the Jacobins and arrest every Jacobin leader he could catch.

The simple idea appealed to a surprising number of legislators, and they retired to consider it. Before they could act, the plan came to the attention of Marie Antoinette, who angrily rejected it. Under no circumstances, she said, did she want to be beholden to Lafayette. His bold plan had to be abandoned, and he returned to Metz after achieving nothing other than the winning of the undying enmity of the Jacobin left.

Lafayette seems to have sensed that worse would follow soon, and he hinted in a letter to Adrienne that it would be wise if she and the children joined him in Metz. Had he ordered her to come she would have obeyed him without question, but a mere suggestion—which may or may not have been an attempt to lull his enemies in the event they intercepted the communication—left the final decision up to her. Adrienne decided her place was at Chavaniac. The nihilistic spirit of the Revolution was spreading from Paris to the provinces, and she was afraid the château would be invaded and sacked if no one stayed behind except her husband's elderly aunt.

Civil war broke out in Paris on August 10, 1792, and a mob attacked the palace, intending to hang the King and Queen. But the Swiss guards held firm, and by the end of the day hundreds on both sides had died. The Jacobins, who had been awaiting their opportunity, seized control of the government. One of their first acts was to order the arrest, return to Paris, and imprisonment of Marshal the Marquis Gilbert de Lafayette.

An officer loyal to Lafayette was the first to reach him with the news. The constitutional monarchy, fragile at best, had collapsed, and the nation had fallen into the hands of conscienceless brigands. Lafayette's first impulse was to drive out the unprincipled rebels, but his own army refused to heed his call. His battalions would not march, and he realized they intended to join the insurrectionists.

These developments created the worst dilemma Lafayette had ever known. He knew that if he did nothing, he would be placed under arrest by commissioners already sent for the purpose, and the Jacobins would hang him or cut off his head in order to intimidate others. And a fight seemed futile. His army was no longer worthy of the name, and might turn on him at any moment. Had he elected to join the King's brothers he would have been welcome, but under no circumstances was he willing to take up arms against France, even though the new government had seized power by illegitimate means.

Lafayette spent the evening of August 14 trying to decide what to do, and at midnight determined to take what he regarded as the least vile of the alternatives open to him. He wrote a short letter to his wife and gave it to a courier, but had no way of knowing whether it would reach her. She did not receive it, and the contents were lost to posterity.

Early on the morning of August 15 Lafayette left his head-quarters, accompanied only by five young staff officers, and rode toward Belgium, which was officially neutral in the war between France and the allied powers. How he managed to pass the sentry outposts without causing an alarm to be raised has never been revealed.

As dawn broke the Hero of Two World crossed the Belgian border and became a refugee from the native land he loved and had served with unselfish distinction.

8

RELATIVES IN PARIS notified Adrienne de Lafayette that the government had ordered her husband's arrest, and she was urged to flee the country. She refused to move until she learned his fate, however, and for days there was no news. Finally, on August 24, she received a letter from her sister Louise de Noailles, telling her he had managed to escape across the border.

Adrienne had no time to rejoice. The messenger who brought her the letter told her that a mob was marching on Chavaniac, intending to burn it to the ground. Her first concern was the safety of her children, and she sent George, with his tutor, to a tiny village near the Swiss border. Calm and methodical, she ordered another carriage to take Anastasie and Virginie to the château at Langeac, which had never been occupied since her husband had bought it several years earlier. Then she burned letters and other documents the Jacobins might regard as proof of treason, and with a courage equal to Lafayette's she awaited the arrival of the mob.

Her unwavering resolve shamed the leaders of the throng, several of whom had been employed on the Lafayette estate, and they neither sacked the château nor burned it. But Adrienne and Charlotte de Chavaniac were forbidden to leave the property, guards were posted outside, and, for all practical purposes, the ladies became prisoners in their own home.

There was still a residue of goodwill toward Lafayette in the district, however. Had he been branded as a refugee from France, his home, belongings, and lands would have been subject to confiscation. But the Jacobin commissioners of Auvergne had longer memories than their colleagues in Paris, and they merely noted in their official reports that the master of Chavaniac was not at home. A slender legal thread enabled Adrienne to retain possession of Chavaniac, at least for the moment.

Meanwhile Lafayette had crossed the border into Belgium and rode toward Holland, where he intended to take passage on a ship to his second country, the United States. He was already a citizen of thirteen states, he owned property there, and, once he found a way to bring his wife and children across the Atlantic, too, he would ride out the storm in the land of liberty.

His plans did not materialize. An Austrian cavalry patrol apprehended him and took him to Namur, where the general in charge of the Austrian garrison, the Marquis de Chasteler, held him in loose confinement pending the arrival of Prince Charles of Lorraine, the cousin of Marie Antoinette.

September 2 was the Day of the Massacres in Paris, and scores of nobles were murdered, among them helpless innocents who had been imprisoned for the crime of their aristocratic birth. The Terror reigned, and the fate of Louis and Marie Antoinette was sealed, their execution certain.

A few days later Adrienne de Lafayette was sent off to prison, along with fifteen-year-old Anastasie, who had been captured at Langeac. Virginie escaped and was hidden by a governess loyal to the family. Charlotte de Chavaniac, against whom no charges had been brought, insisted on going to jail with her nephew's wife.

Meanwhile Lafayette was encountering unexpected difficulties of his own. Prince Charles assumed that the Marquis would be cooperative and tell him in detail about the size, strength, and disposition of the French forces gathered across the border. Lafayette, to his amazement, would reveal nothing.

His sense of honor intact, Lafayette made his position clear. He granted that he had been forced to flee for his life and had been shamefully treated by the Jacobins who had seized control of his country. But he was convinced their rule would last only a short time, and under no circumstances would he betray the nation whose uniform he still wore.

Uncertain how to handle this strange man to whom honor was all-important, Prince Charles transferred him to a small castle at nearby Nivelle. There he would remain until the Emperor Joseph received a full report on the matter in Vienna and personally decided his fate.

Lafayette wrote a long letter to Adrienne, which she received only a few hours before her own arrest. In it he expressed confidence that she and the children would join him in the immediate future, as not even Jacobins waged civil war against women and children. He believed his own difficulties were caused by misunderstandings, and he was confident the Emperor soon would release him. Then he and his family would go to England to visit relatives who had previously left France, and thereafter they would sail to the United States.

Lafayette's ingenuousness at this critical time in his life is as amazing as his sense of honor. Obviously he had no under-standing of the world of real politics. The regime of the Em-peror Joseph was the most reactionary in Europe, and although Lafayette had been received at court in Vienna, neither the monarch nor members of his administration admired a man whose concepts of liberty and equality had been at least partly responsible, in their opinion, for the current upheavals in France. Lafayette might be the darling of liberals everywhere, but he represented a distinct threat to the security of a regime that used severe repression to hold together an empire whose people lived in many nations, spoke their own languages, and followed their own customs.

Equally important, Joseph was the brother of Marie An-toinette, and had received letter after letter from her damning the officer she held to blame for her imprisonment. She hadn't understood that he had been sincere in protecting her life with his own, and in her correspondence with her brother she had referred to him as "the jailer."

Now she was in grave danger, and there was nothing Joseph could do to save her. The Emperor, who was endowed with many of the faults and few of the virtues of the Hapsburgs, was arrogant and narrow-minded, shortsighted in his determina-tion to maintain the status quo at all costs, and personally vindictive. He regarded it as a stroke of fate that the man Marie Antoinette held responsible for her troubles had fallen into his hands.

Lafayette was taken to Prussia and confined in the old for-tress of Spandau.

Adrienne, her elder daughter, and her husband's aunt were released from prison and returned to the château at Chavaniac, where they promised to stay. Guards were stationed outside, but most had been Lafayette's admirers, and looked the other way when Adrienne corresponded with George and Virginie, who remained in hiding. The Terror had not yet reached out for women with the severity with which it dealt with men, and she recognized her son's danger. He was Lafayette's principal heir, and would be imprisoned in Lafayette's place if the new regime caught him. Adrienne conceived the idea of sending the boy to the United States, where Washington was president and Jefferson a member of the Cabinet. There he would be safe, and she began to plan accordingly.

On September 22 the monarchy was dissolved, and France became a republic.

A decree abolished the nobility, including titles of rank, and everyone in France became a citizen.

Citizen Gilbert Lafayette was declared an enemy of France and condemned to death in absentia. His property was confiscated, his commission as a general was rescinded, and all honors he had received were canceled.

Adrienne wrote to President Washington, asking him to use his influence to obtain her husband's release. Remembering that Lafayette had visited Frederick II, she sent that monarch a letter, urging him to release her husband. Gouverneur Morris, still the American minister to France, privately supplied her with cash. She sent George off on the first leg of his journey, to England, and the arrangements were so secret that she did not even see her son to bid him a final farewell before he was smuggled out of France.

Again Lafayette was transferred, this time to a castle at Wesel in Westphalia. As he was moved nearer to Austria, the Emperor Joseph became increasingly nervous, and the prisoner was refused the right to receive visitors or to send or receive mail. He was separated from his aides, his guard detail was doubled, and an attempt was made to place him in chains. But his icy outrage so intimidated the warden of the castle that the effort was abandoned. If Joseph and his subordinates learned that Lafayette had been proscribed in France, stripped of his property, and condemned to death, they gave no sign of it. They regarded him as their natural enemy, too. The French sought his life because he was too royalist; the Austrians kept him imprisoned because he was too antiroyalist.

Lafayette's friends became active, but there was little they could do. President Washington wrote personally to the Emperor, requesting Lafayette's release, and Secretary of State Jefferson ordered the entire American diplomatic corps to work toward that same end. But the United States was a young, feeble nation, totally lacking in influence in central Europe, and the requests were ignored.

Nowhere did Lafayette's plight arouse greater sympathy than in Great Britain, where men of every political persuasion clamored for his release. Austria turned a deaf ear to these entreaties also.

In December 1792 Adrienne Lafayette was ordered released from arrest. President Washington immediately placed a sum of money at her disposal in Amsterdam so that she and her family could travel to the United States, but she was not permitted to leave France. She was allowed to continue to live at Chavaniac, but was totally without funds; family servants, many of whom had served her since childhood, continued to work for her without pay.

On January 21, 1793, Citizen Louis Capet, formerly His Christian Majesty Louis XVI, was executed in Paris. The entire civilized world recoiled in horror when this simple man, foolish but harmless, died on the guillotine. The Terror became worse, and it was only a matter of time before Marie Antoinette would die too.

The Allies intensified their military efforts, but the citizen armies of France surprised their enemies and themselves by holding their own. Their relative success was due less to their own valor and skill than to the ineptitude of the Austrian and refugee French generals who opposed them. Meanwhile for mer nobles were being imprisoned and executed by the hundreds in Paris and elsewhere. No aristocratic family was safe, no family escaped the Terror.

Lafayette, who knew literally nothing of what was taking place in the outside world, sent a strongly worded petition to the Emperor, demanding his freedom on the grounds that he was a citizen of the United States. Joseph did not deign to reply, but Lafayette's warden informed him that since he had been wearing the uniform of a French marshal when he had been captured, he would be treated like a Frenchman.

In February 1793 he was transferred again, this time to Magdeburg. His family had no idea what had become of him, and he did not know if his wife and children were alive or dead. He was allowed to read books, but the blank pages were torn out so that he could not use them for writing paper, and he was not permitted a pen. In March, however, he obtained paper and ink from a friendly jailer, and using a toothpick as a pen he wrote to Adrienne's relative the Princesse d'Hénin, an intellectual who shared his liberal views and who had escaped from the Terror to London. Showing remarkably little emotion, he told her in detail about his confinement, his inadequate meals, and the filth of his tiny cell.

The Princesse d'Hénin made the letter public, much to the embarrassment of the Emperor. Through friends in England, Adrienne learned her husband was alive, so the most severe of her worries was ended. She wrote to him, and her letter, after passing through many hands, was finally delivered to him by

Charles de Damas, his former aide and the brother of Diane de Simiane. Damas was now a refugee.

Virginie emerged from hiding and joined her mother at Chavaniac. George and his tutor reached the United States, and word of their safe arrival finally came to Adrienne after many delays.

Early in October Lafayette managed to write a brief letter to his wife and found a courier willing to smuggle it out of the Magdeburg fortress for him. She received it early in November. It was the first direct word she had received from him since he had vanished.

Soon thereafter her own troubles multiplied. Robespierre and his colleagues continued to regard Lafayette as one of the most prominent of France's enemies, and his wife was too much in the public eye to permit her to retain her freedom. No formal charges were placed against her, but none were necessary under the Terror, and she was arrested and taken off to the crowded jail in the little town of Brioude.

Adrienne regarded herself as fortunate. On October 16 Marie Antoinette lost her life, and three weeks later the Duc d'Orléans, who had made the mistake of returning to France from exile, was also guillotined. The pace of executions increased. Former nobles, intellectuals, moderates whose only sin was their hatred of violence, and others of every political persuasion were killed. Although Adrienne did not yet know it, her mother and her elder sister, Louise de Noailles, had been arrested and imprisoned.

Late in May 1794 an order suddenly reached Brioude transferring Citizeness Lafayette to Paris. She assured her daughters, who paid her a tearful farewell visit, that she had not lost hope; she was being sent to a jail for ordinary criminals rather than one of the former palaces whose inmates rarely left except for the trip to the guillotine, and she had not been summoned to appear before the Tribunal of the Revolution, which was tantamount to a death sentence.

By this time all of Lafayette's properties had been sold at auction for small sums of money. The new owners of Chavaniac, apparently embarrassed because of the high regard in which his former employees, tenants, and neighbors still held him, permitted his aunt and daughters to live in a small apartment in one wing of the château.

At least seventy-five victims were being claimed by the guillotine each day, and among them in the summer of 1794 were Adrienne Lafayette's mother, sister, and grandmother. It seemed inevitable that she, too, soon would mount the scaffold. Others were being murdered only because of their noble birth, but she was the wife of an aristocrat whose name was remembered with abiding affection by hundreds of thousands of citizens. Such dangerous persons had to be destroyed.

Word of her imprisonment in Paris reached Gouverneur Morris a short time before he was replaced as United States minister to France by James Monroe. Morris reacted promptly to the challenge, and writing a strong protest, he presented it in person to Robespierre, now the nation's dictator. The entire Lafayette family, he declared, was dear to the people of America, and if Adrienne Lafayette lost her life to the guillotine the relations of the United States with France, her first and dearest ally, would be severely harmed. The President, his cabinet, the Congress, and the American people would regard her execution as a deliberately unfriendly act that might force the termination of the treaties of alliance and trade that bound the two nations.

Morris had not checked with the State Department before writing his letter, but undoubtedly knew it would meet with the complete approval of President Washington. Certainly the public repercussions would have been strong, too, if Adrienne had been murdered by the bloodthirsty zealots who were using the Terror as an instrument of government.

Robespierre and his immediate associates made no reply, either in a formal communication or in conversation, but they were nevertheless deeply impressed. The coalition of powers opposed to France was growing, and the ranks of neutrals were being thinned by the Terror, which convinced conservatives and liberals, monarchists and republicans everywhere that the French were indulging in inexcusable barbarism. The United States was France's only friend, and was needed as an anchor for the French possessions in the Caribbean.

With so many people being executed and horror so prevalent, the saving of one life did not seem too high a price to pay for friendship. Thanks to Morris' timely intervention, the life of Adrienne Lafayette was spared. She was not notified of this decision, however, and her jailers allowed her to drift from day to day, never knowing when she might be called to the tumbril that would carry her to her execution.

In the autumn of 1794 Monroe, the new American minister, made heroic efforts to win Adrienne's release from prison, but this could not be accomplished. The government thought it had already been generous, but as a further gesture intended to placate the Americans, she was moved to a somewhat less crowded prison.

There she suffered in stoic silence. The food was almost inedible, the cold was penetrating, and she had inadequate clothing and blankets to ward off the chill. But she made no complaint, and even her jailers were impressed.

Meanwhile men of compassion in Great Britain and the United States were creating such a furor about the incarceration of Lafayette that the Prussians decided to get rid of their unwelcome guest and turned him over to the Austrians. He was moved, in the early autumn of 1794, to an old fortress at Olmütz.

The conditions of his imprisonment became much more harsh. He was held in solitary confinement, given no opportunity to exercise in the stone-enclosed courtyard of the fortress, and forbidden to send or receive letters. He was given no medication when he suffered from bronchitis, and a physician was summoned only when it was feared he might die, which would have embarrassed Austria. The Emperor, unable to understand what had been happening in France and unwilling to learn, continued to hold Lafayette personally responsible for the death of his sister. Members of the Cabinet, afraid the new French disease would spread to Austria, saw in Lafayette all that was corrupt and savage in Paris. Their armies were unable to punish the regiments of the First Republic, but this man who was personally responsible for Europe's woes was their prisoner, and they could not treat him with enough severity.

One man more than any other refused to accept the injustices being inflicted on the Lafayettes. The austere, high-principled James Monroe, the future fifth president of the United States, was outraged and felt compelled to act accordingly. He bombarded the Emperor with letters, and wrote repeatedly to members of the Austrian government, demanding the immediate release of Lafayette. He was somewhat more diplomatic in his attempts to win Adrienne's freedom, but the effects were the same. His correspondence inundated French officials who were in a position to set Citizeness Lafayette free.

Neither of his persistent campaigns bore immediate fruit. "The very name of Lafayette inspires fear in the Ministries here," he wrote to President Washington. "The rulers are afraid his mere appearance in the streets of Paris would rally the people to the cause of liberty and drive them out of office."

Suddenly, on January 21, 1795, Adrienne Lafayette was released from prison. She was granted her freedom without warning, and was told only that all charges against her, none of which she had ever learned, had been dropped. She went immediately to the house of the American minister, where Monroe and his wife, Elizabeth, nursed her back to health.

While there she learned for the first time that her husband had been moved to Olmütz and that he was being treated with extraordinary severity. She also heard about a romantic attempt that had been made to rescue him. The Princesse d'Hénin, in London, had raised money for the purpose, and the effort had been made by two dedicated young men. One was a German physician named Bollman, and the other was the son of Major Huger of the South Carolina militia, at whose house Lafayette had stayed on his first night in America.

The pair had actually succeeded in smuggling Lafayette out of Olmütz, a remarkable feat, but young Huger's inability to speak German had betrayed them. Lafayette had been recaptured, returned to Olmütz, and placed in even stricter solitary confinement under an augmented guard. Newspapers, especially in the United States, Great Britain, Holland, and Sweden, soon printed accounts of the incident, none of them accurate and most exaggerated. The Emperor Joseph and members of his entourage were unable to understand why the fate of one former French noble should arouse such a furor. "Sad to relate," the *Times* of London said in an editorial, "His Majesty does not understand the meaning or essence of human freedoms. Not even the vicious execution of his sister in France has served to enlighten him."

Adrienne Lafayette for the first time expressed aloud an idea she had been mulling over during her own imprisonment. She wanted to join her husband and share his captivity with him. If possible she would take her daughters with her, and the entire family, save for George, would be reunited.

The Monroes thought the idea insane, and advised against it. So did Adrienne's sister Pauline de Montagu, who was living in exile in Germany. Aware of Adrienne's stubborn streak when she had made up her mind, Pauline offered her practical advice: When traveling, she said, Adrienne should not use her own name because the authorities might halt her. But Lafayette was so highly regarded by people throughout Europe that many would come to the aid of his wife.

Other forces were already in motion. In London a committee was formed under the unofficial chairmanship of the Princesse d'Hénin to win Lafayette's release. A similar organization was formed in the United States, and thousands subscribed to it. The French were unable to act in the open, but scores of Lafayette's friends and admirers came privately to Adrienne and offered whatever help and support they could give.

The campaign swiftly gained momentum. Charles Fox, one of the most prominent political leaders in England, took an active part in the cause, even though Prime Minister Pitt was determined to take no action that might disturb his country's precarious alliance with Austria. Editorials appeared in many British and American newspapers, and the cry "Liberty for Lafayette!" was picked up by the press of Germany and Switzerland.

The Emperor Joseph gave no indication that he read one word. It is possible that he was ignorant of the campaign, but even if he learned of it, he saw no reason to recognize the clamor. He was determined to avenge the death of his sister, and Lafayette remained the object of that vengeance.

The man whose fate was of growing concern on two continents was in surprisingly good spirits. He engaged in daily physical exercises in the confines of his cramped cell in order to stay fit, and he read incessantly. The Hapsburgs entertained a low opinion of the written word, so he was permitted to read as much as he pleased, and books preserved his sanity.

He also sharpened his wits by finding ways to outsmart his jailers, inventing ruses to obtain paper and ink, then smuggling out letters. Shortly after Adrienne's release from prison she received two short letters from him, both forwarded to her through illegal channels by Pauline de Montagu.

Perhaps the most extraordinary aspect of the saga of Gilbert and Adrienne Lafayette was their conviction, joint and separate, that they would surmount their difficulties. Both believed their good name and property would be restored. Both felt certain that the present insanity in France would pass and that the Hero of Two Worlds would be given another major role to play in his country's destiny. Adrienne was buoyed by the certain knowledge that her husband was one of the great men of the age, and he shared that belief. Their present sufferings were no more than a preparation for a return to a useful, productive life as a leader of France. Not even the damp darkness of the dungeon cell to which Lafayette had been moved could shake his view, which his wife shared.

9

SHORTLY AFTER Adrienne Lafayette's release from prison she held a reunion with Diane de Simiane, who also had spent many months in jail. Both women had lost many of their relatives and most of their property, but neither referred to her problems, and they made great efforts to keep up their spirits. Adrienne confided her plan to join her husband at the first opportunity, and promised to give him Diane's love.

Late in the winter of 1795 Adrienne went to Chavaniac, where she was reunited with her daughters, and soon thereafter she was joined by another of her sisters, Rosalie de Grammont. Only the Lafayettes had dropped the noble "de" from their name.

By the spring of 1795 it was gradually becoming evident that the Terror had ended and moderate elements had gained control of the government. Street mobs were disbanded; the National Guard was reorganized, and only reliable men were permitted to serve. The nation's finances were in a chaotic state, and the new rulers, in one of their first moves to restore order, decided to restore properties illegally wrested from people of substance.

Adrienne Lafayette immediately set out for Paris, accompanied by her daughters and her sister. She and Rosalie de Grammont applied for the lands and homes they had inherited from their murdered mother, and when they won their suit Adrienne promptly applied for restoration of Chavaniac and numerous other properties. The name of Lafayette was no longer anathema to the authorities, and her petition was granted. It might be a long time before these properties again produced revenues, but the base of the Lafayette fortunes had been restored, and at the very least Gilbert's elderly aunt could live without fear at Chavaniac, the only home she had ever known.

At the beginning of August 1795, Adrienne Lafayette at last was granted passports for herself and her daughters. Once again James Monroe had intervened, and the documents gave her the right to travel with her children to the United States. She had not been given the right to visit Germany and Austria, but she had been through too much to quibble about mere technicalities. The Germans and Austrians would not be picayune, and once she left France the authorities there wouldn't know her destination.

Showing remarkable financial acumen, she put her husband's business affairs and her own in order. Farmers were being encouraged to raise crops again, and she borrowed hard cash so the peasants of Chavaniac could return to their labors. After attending to these matters she went off to Dunkirk with Anastasie and Virginie, staying at the home of the United States consul there, and on September 5, 1795, the trio boarded an American packet ostensibly bound for New York. Instead, by prearrangement, it sailed to Hamburg.

Refugee relatives living outside Hamburg took in Adrienne and her children, and she was reunited with her sister Pauline. The American consul in Hamburg cooperated with the wife of Lafayette, as his colleague in Dunkirk had done, and passports were issued to a Mrs. Motier of Hartford, Connecticut, and her children, granting them the right to travel through Germany and Austria. The way was at last clear for Adrienne to make her way to her husband's side. Funds supplied by the American consul even enabled her to buy a carriage and a team of horses, and she also hired a coachman and a ladies' maid. After her years of hardship and imprisonment, she reclaimed what she regarded as her right to live and travel like a lady of means.

In late April 1795 Adrienne and her daughters reached Vienna. The Emperor had died and had been succeeded by his son, Francis II, a young man of considerable charm and limited intelligence who listened to the members of his father's cabinet, all of whom he had retained in office. Adrienne took lodgings as Mrs. Motier.

Most of Europe's noblemen were related by blood or marriage, and Adrienne had no difficulty in getting in touch with a cousin, who made an appointment for her with the court chamberlain. She revealed her true identity to him and told him the purpose of her presence in the city, and he, in turn, presented her to the chancellor, Baron von Thugut.

Her request placed the Austrian government in a quandary. If she and her two attractive daughters were granted permission to share Lafayette's imprisonment, the pressures to release him would grow greater everywhere. If her request were denied, however, Austria would appear in the eyes of the world as barbaric and unfeeling. The chancellor arranged for an audience with the Emperor, privately advising Francis to grant her wish and hope the world soon would forget the family Lafayette.

Adrienne took advantage of her meeting with the Emperor to ask for her husband's release. Francis said he was sorry, but the terms of his alliance with Great Britain and Prussia made this impossible. Inasmuch as his treaties with those nations were secret documents, their terms never having been revealed, Adrienne had no way of knowing whether he was telling the truth or hiding behind an excuse. So she asked for the right to join Lafayette.

Even though Francis had been warned, her request jolted him, and he questioned her at length. Did she know the difficulties, unpleasantnesses, and inconveniences of prison life? She replied with great dignity that she had spent many months as the prisoner of the Committee of Public Safety in France.

The discomfited emperor granted her and her daughters the right to join the former marquis, and before the audience ended he impulsively told her she could get in direct personal touch with him at any time she might wish. Presumably he reasoned that she would grow tired of incarceration in the old fortress and soon would want to be released.

After many delays, most of them intended to discourage the determined woman, she and her daughters were granted a "permit of incarceration," a document unlike any other in the history of the empire. Adrienne and the girls traveled to Olmütz, arriving there on the afternoon of October 15, 1795, and were conducted to Lafayette's cell.

Lafayette was painfully thin, had lost much of his hair, and had aged far beyond his thirty-eight years. Adrienne's own ordeal had turned her hair gray. Anastasie had become a young woman since her father had last seen her, and even Virginia, no longer a small child, was mature and poised.

Until the moment his family entered his cell Lafayette had not known for certain whether they were dead or alive. He had heard vague reports of the Terror in France, but the history of recent years was all new to him, and he was shocked to learn of the death of Adrienne's mother, sister, and grandmother, and of so many other relatives and lifelong friends.

The cell adjoining Lafayette's was opened for Adrienne and the girls, and they were given two cots for three people. Adrienne received no reply to her request to attend mass once each week. She and the girls, like Lafayette, were given no silverware, and were compelled to eat their meals with their fingers.

But these were minor inconveniences; other conditions were frightful. The guards' latrines were located a short distance from the twin cells, and the stench was almost unbearable. An open sewer passed beneath the high, barred windows, and the prisoners were forced to suffer infestations of insects during the warm months of the year. Lights were extinguished promptly at nine each night, and the lamps were removed until morning. There was more than enough to eat—Adrienne paid for their meals with cash—but the food, she wrote, was "indescribably filthy." She and her daughters were separated from Lafayette at night, and were locked into their own cell until 8:00 A.M., when they were permitted to join him for the day. The fortress physician spoke no French and the Lafayette family's knowledge of German was limited, so Lafayette communicated with him in Latin. This was permitted provided an officer who understood the language was present. If one did not happen to be on hand, the visits of the physician were delayed, no matter how urgently his presence might be needed.

The buoyancy of the girls enabled their parents to withstand the ordeal. Virginie was a natural mimic, and teased the officers of the garrison, the soldiers, and the guards without mercy. Often they became infuriated, but were afraid to strike her. Anastasie treated the entire staff with a lofty contempt that also annoyed them, and delighted in laughing at them to their faces. Now eighteen, she was endowed with her parents' good looks, and she made it her business to become friendly with a number of sentries. Now she could buy candy, ink, paper, and other treasures from them, even though they could be beaten for their derelictions when they broke the rules. At thirteen Virginie was irrepressible, and her antics so amused the staff, including the assistant commandant, that she was responsible for the "mail service," which enabled her parents to send out letters notifying relatives and friends of their situation.

Lafayette's health improved dramatically after his family's arrival at Olmütz. He gained no weight, but his spirits soared and he began to think about the future again. He seemed to grow younger each day, at least in his wife's eyes, and his energies, previously almost inexhaustible, soon were restored. His recuperative powers were remarkable.

Adrienne was not in good health, however, and her present imprisonment, combined with what she had suffered in France, depleted her. She suffered from severe headaches that no medication could cure, and in a number of letters smuggled out and ultimately received by members of her family she complained of "bad blood." Her husband repeatedly urged her to leave him, which she was at liberty to do, but she indignantly refused. She did not think of herself as a heroine, nor did she regard what she was doing as making a sacrifice. She believed he needed her, and under no circumstances was she willing to be separated from him again.

Several other French noblemen also were being held as prisoners at Olmütz, and the Lafayette girls soon devised an ingenious method of communicating with them. Anastasie had a clear singing voice, and, making up tunes, she sang them the news in French slang. She established a code system with them, and thereafter they communicated by tapping on the stones at their windows. The jailers knew something of the sort was happening, but had little control over the practice. Thanks to Anastasie and Virginie, the morale of the Olmütz garrison declined.

In the spring of 1796 Adrienne sent a letter to the Emperor, asking for permission to visit Vienna for a period of ten days to see a physician there. Francis replied through a member of his household staff that she had requested the right to share her husband's imprisonment, and that she would be permitted to leave Olmütz only if she did not return there. She refused to consider the proposal and wrote a blistering reply in a cramped hand, her fingers having become so swollen that she could scarcely hold a pen.

It did not occur to the Emperor and his staff that they had blundered in permitting Adrienne and her daughters to join Lafayette, or that they were compounding their error by the harsh terms of the family's imprisonment. Members of the American diplomatic corps worked hard to obtain the release of the Lafayettes, and American public opinion was strongly anti-Austrian. The "Lafayette party" in England grew and became more vocal, and even the most conservative Tories were finding it difficult to excuse the behavior of Britain's ally.

Moderates were now in control of the government in France, where people of every persuasion, whether they had approved of Lafayette or had hated him, were becoming increasingly indignant about his harsh imprisonment by France's enemy. A new star was rising in 1796, however, a General Napoleon Bonaparte having been given command of the army that was being sent into Italy. He pictured himself as a man on horseback, and he wanted no competition from a man whose exploits when riding his white horse were legendary.

The basic military situation was complicated, to say the least. Many of the Italian states belonged to Austria, and it was these territories that Bonaparte set out to liberate. His campaign made the Austrians all the more determined to hold Lafayette, his compatriot, in prison.

This would not be the last time that Napoleon's ambitions would be harmful to Lafayette. Their subsequent careers ran parallel to each other with the inexorable persistence of a Greek tragedy.

The Corsican-born Bonaparte, once a corporal, was one of the true geniuses of history, perhaps the greatest of all Frenchmen. It was Lafayette's misfortune to be his contemporary.

Letters smuggled into Olmütz indicated that members of the Directory, as the new five-man ruling body in France was called, clung to the belief that Lafayette was a royalist who favored the return of the Comte de Provence, Louis XVI's brother. This was of course untrue, and Lafayette went to work to set the record straight. He dictated letters, refraining from writing them himself because the guards would recognize his handwriting even if they did not understand French, and would destroy the communications. Adrienne wrote when her ailments permitted, and sometimes Anastasie took down her father's words.

Soon the Directory was being bombarded with General Lafayette's views. He had long favored republican principles, as anyone acquainted with his American experiences well knew, and had been loyal to the crown only because he had taken an oath to serve the King. Every letter stressed that he had no desire to upset the present political balance in France.

Bonaparte created a sensation in May of 1796, sweeping the enemies of France before him and winning impressive victories over the supposedly invincible legions of Austria. The presence of the prewar French general and his family at Olmütz was becoming a source of increasing embarrassment for the Emperor.

In that same month President Washington, restraining his personal indignation sufficiently to write diplomatically, sent a letter to Francis II in which he said that he and the American people would be eternally grateful if Lafayette, his wife, and their daughters were released. Gouverneur Morris, still in Europe, got in touch with the Austrian chancellor, who admitted the probability that the Lafayettes would be released as soon as the campaign in Italy ended. The Austrian government did not wish to appear to be giving in to outside pressures.

At the end of 1796 a new element entered into the situation. Adrienne's health was declining, and the fortress physician reported that she might die if she were not released. The Austrian government made an attempt to pry her away from her husband's side, but she refused to be moved. Francis II had to contemplate the reactions of the world if "the heroine of Olmütz," as newspapers throughout Europe were now calling her, did not survive.

Certainly her sacrifice had called the attention of people everywhere to her husband's plight. Poems were written about her, songs were sung. Mme de Staël wrote to Adrienne that the pressures being exerted on the Austrian government were becoming unbearable.

General Bonaparte exerted some pressures of his own, and they were even more convincing. By 1797 his armies had won Italy, and were threatening to invade the heart of the Austrian Empire. It was conceivable that he could even take Vienna, and the Austrians sued for peace, leaving their British ally stranded.

Napoleon Bonaparte was now strong enough to be generous

to a fellow Frenchman he no longer regarded as a threat to his own ambitions. Besides, he was a true patriot, and found the incarceration of Lafayette and other French officers galling. One of his peace terms was the immediate release of all French prisoners held in Austria. Their freedom, as one member of the Directory declared, had become "a matter of national honor second to none."

During the long months of negotiation between victor and vanquished, conditions at Olmütz changed. The Lafayettes were allowed to mingle with other prisoners and to exercise in the courtyard. The doors between the Lafayettes' cells were left unlocked at night, and the captives expected to be set free at any time. Adrienne wrote to her sisters and to Diane de Simiane that she hoped to see all of them in the near future.

Neither Lafayette nor his wife seemed to realize they were valuable pawns in the long and painful negotiations the Austrians were conducting with General Bonaparte. Their ultimate release was certain, but their captors tried to win concessions from the conqueror of Italy in return for granting them their freedom, and the talks dragged on for months.

The actual terms of the peace treaty, as they were finally drawn, specified that General Lafayette would be freed and expelled from the Austrian Empire. The wording also made clear that, at least for the present, he was not to be returned to France. Who was responsible for this curious clause has been something of a mystery for almost two centuries.

The startled Lafayette suspected the provision was inserted by Bonaparte, who wanted no rival in his accelerating bid for power and had no desire to compete with a hero who was wearing the wreath of a martyr. The victory of the French over the Austrians had excited and pleased Lafayette, and he was still proud of his compatriots' achievements, but for the first time he realized that Napoleon Bonaparte might represent a new danger.

Late in July 1797, three months after the end of military hostilities, the Emperor finally sent an envoy to Olmütz with word that the Lafayettes would be granted their immediate freedom on the condition that the General gave his formal, unconditional promise never again to set foot on Austrian soil.

At first Lafayette tried to pass off the demand as a joke, saying he failed to see how one enfeebled, underweight man could threaten the mighty empire. The emissary made it clear that the condition was absolute and that the pledge had to be made in writing.

This touched Lafayette on the most sensitive of his nerves, his honor. He said that he had no desire ever to come to Austria again, particularly after the way he had been treated there. If left to his own devices he would gladly give the promise. But he was not his own master. He was a citizen of France, and if ordered to return to Austria in his country's service he would be compelled to obey.

The emissary went back to Vienna, and the Lafayettes remained in prison. Adrienne applauded the stand her husband had taken, and so did their daughters. Honor was more important to the family than liberty or even life itself.

General Bonaparte was annoyed by the position Lafayette had taken. The Hero of Two Worlds was being applauded in Paris for his high principles, and men who had known him in his days of glory were speaking of his being given a place in the government.

The Austrians were exasperated. They wanted to be rid of their unwelcome prisoners, but it was obvious they would not be able to persuade Lafayette to change his mind. In desperation they decided to utilize a different approach: They would send the Lafayette family to Hamburg, turn them over to the United States consul there, and request him to ship them off to America. A man with Lafayette's ideas of freedom was too dangerous to be left at large in Europe.

In a final attempt to avoid the unpleasant publicity that would be certain to follow the Lafayettes' revelations of the conditions of their imprisonment, the Austrians tried to persuade them to make a statement to the effect that the jailers at Olmütz were personally responsible for the hardships they had endured there. The Austrian government would punish these officials, and would be absolved of guilt. Lafayette, speaking for the family, not only refused but expressed the conviction that the jailers at Olmütz were blameless and had been following orders emanating from the highest authority.

Worn down and unwilling to quibble any longer with this impossible man, the Austrians gave up. On the morning of September 19, 1797, Gilbert Lafayette, his wife, and their daughters walked out of the fortress in which they had been confined. As a "gift" of the Emperor they were provided with new clothes. Lafayette's boots were the first real footgear he had worn in two years, his jailers having refused to allow him to replace the shoes that had worn out. He and Adrienne instantly understood the reason for the Austrians' seeming generosity: They didn't want their former captives traveling across Europe in rags.

A cavalry escort surrounded the carriage, and the Lafayettes soon realized they were not truly free. They were given no voice in the selection of the itinerary that would take them to Hamburg, and they were allowed virtually no contact with any friends or relatives on their journey. The party did not travel in anonymity, however. In Dresden, Leipzig, and Halle huge crowds gathered to cheer the Hero of Two Worlds, and prominent liberal leaders pushed through the cavalry cordon to shake Lafayette's hand. He loved these demonstrations of his undiminished popularity, and he and his daughters rapidly lost their prison pallor, regained their appetites, and recovered their strength. Adrienne continued to suffer from headaches, dizziness, and swollen joints, but made no complaint.

On October 4 the party arrived in Hamburg, and thousands of citizens lined the streets to welcome the renowned prisoners of Olmütz. A formal ceremony was held at the house of the American consul, with an Austrian official handing the Lafayettes over to him. The captivity at last came to an end.

Gouverneur Morris, who was present, believed he had been responsible for the family's release, and they thanked him for his efforts, but they knew that the success of French arms against the Austrians actually had opened the gates of their jail. Thirty-six hours after arriving in Hamburg Lafayette wrote a letter to Bonaparte:

> Citizen General, the prisoners of Olmütz, happy in the knowledge that they owe their freedom to the irresistible might of your soldiers, found consolation while still in captivity in the realization that their lives and liberties were bound up with the triumphs of the Republic and with your own personal glory. They are no less happy today to pay homage to their liberator. . . . It is from the place where we have paid a last farewell to our jailers that we send our messages of gratitude to their conqueror. . . .
> In our remote refuge on the Danish territory of Holstein,

where we shall try to reestablish that health which you have saved, we join with our patriotic wishes for the success of the Republic expressions of the strongest possible concern for the illustrious general to whom we are the more strongly attached by reason of the services he has rendered to the cause of liberty and of our country. The gratitude which we delight in owing him is graven forever on our hearts.

The first order of business was that of determining where to stay, and Lafayette was making no long-range decision. Until he gained a clearer picture of the political situation in France, where various republican factions were engaged in a power struggle, he had no intention of committing himself to a permanent life in the United States. He learned that the present members of the Directory did not look with favor on his return to Paris, but he wanted the dust to settle before he made up his mind.

His immediate concern was the health of his wife, who was too ill to make the long voyage to the United States. Adrienne's aunt the Comtesse de Tesse, who had escaped from France with most of her fortune prior to the Terror, owned an estate near Hamburg, outside a village called Witmold, and invited the Lafayettes to visit her for as long as they cared to stay.

During the few days Lafayette remained in Hamburg the outside world descended on him and tried to take advantage of his renown. French royalists urged him to declare his allegiance to the refugee Comte de Provence, whom they were calling Louis XVIII, and they assured him he would hold a high place at court when the Bourbon dynasty was restored. He was similarly besieged by the liberal Republicans, who felt uneasy over the growing power of Bonaparte and wanted to counter his influence under the banner of the returned hero-martyr.

Lafayette was courteous to both groups, but refused to make any commitments for the present. Instead, after a stay of less than a week in Hamburg, he went off with his wife and daughters to the estate of the Comtesse de Tesse.

10

Witmold was an enormous estate, its principal buildings occupied by many members of the Noailles-Ayen families who had gone into exile. Thanks to the energies of Mme de Tesse the place was self-sustaining, her crops and dairy products bringing in a large income. The Lafayettes were given a warm welcome, and felt they had at last come home. Anastasie and Virginie were taken into the circle of their many cousins, and soon put the horrors of Olmütz out of their minds. Adrienne was pampered by her relatives, in spite of her protests, and was allowed to do little for herself. Her husband immediately fitted into his role as the senior male member of the household. It was difficult for his younger relatives, who hadn't seen him since they were children, to realize he was only forty years old.

In a letter to a friend his sister-in-law, Pauline de Montague described his return from the dead:

Monsieur de La Fayette was quickly apprised of all that had happened since he had, in a sense, disappeared from the world.

He was so little changed that, listening to him, one felt oneself grow young again. He was still as he had been all his life. He showed no bitterness, no hatred of persons or of parties, but there was not the smallest change in his opinions. He felt neither regret nor reproach in his political conscience for any of his actions, for any of his words, for any of his thoughts. With him one was always at the Declaration of the Rights of Man and the dawn of the Revolution. Everything else was just a great misfortune, a tissue of accidents, deplorable, no doubt, but not in his opinion any more discouraging than stories of shipwreck are to good sailors. He had the simple-minded faith and the calm fearlessness of those old navigators who in the sixteenth century set out to explore the world in ill-equipped ships with mutinous crews. He was prepared to go aboard again. . . .

In a letter to her sister Rosalie de Grammont, Pauline spoke even more bluntly:

Gilbert is just as good, just as simple, just as affectionate, just as sweet-tempered in argument as when you knew him first. He loves his children and in spite of his cold exterior is charming with his wife. He has an affable manner, an imperturbability by which I am not taken in, and a secret longing for action within his power to direct and control. I avoid, so far as is possible, talking to him about anything that has to do with the Revolution, both what he defends and what he condemns in it. I am afraid of losing my temper, and also of hurting him. I see with pleasure that those around me approve of my attitude of reserve. To be patient, and not to become involved, that is my rule of conduct where he is concerned. . . .

Poor Gilbert, may God preserve him from ever again playing a part on the political stage.

In his own mind Lafayette quickly made the transition from the Europe he had left in 1792 to the new era of 1797. But almost everyone who conversed with him, other than his adoring wife, realized he had not really brought himself up to date. He felt contempt for the royalists, which he took care to express only to a few intimates; he was suspicious of Bonaparte; and he believed the current rulers of the Republic were subverting the natural rights of man while paying lip service to liberty. Nevertheless he felt his usual optimism, and waited with confidence for a change in the political climate that would enable him to mount his white horse again.

He was too proud to stay for more than a limited time as the guest of his wife's aunt. Thanks to Adrienne's efforts on his behalf before she left France to join him in prison, he enjoyed moderately sound finances, and after a few weeks at Witmold he leased a château called Lemkuhlen, about an hour's hard ride from the Tesse property. He and his family moved in with his aides, their wives and children, and a large staff of servants. Since he had not known the disasters that had befallen other wealthy aristocrats during the early years of the Revolution, it did not occur to him to live modestly.

The move was made early in November, and Lafayette promptly embarked on a new regimen. For the sake of his health he went off for an hour's canter every morning before breakfast, and, frequently feeling the need for more exercise, he felled trees in the woods behind the château and cut them up for firewood. Each day he worked on his memoirs and made extensive notes for what he hoped would become a comprehensive history of the times through which he had lived. His correspondence was extensive, and he received thousands of letters from well-wishers in many lands. He made it his business to answer every communication, an endless task, and he also wrote frequently to Diane de Simiane. Before night fell he went off for another canter, sometimes accompanied by his daughters and his aides. His evenings were spent at Adrienne's bedside, where he usually read to her until she fell asleep.

Some of Lafayette's estates had not yet been restored to him, and he wanted to go to Paris to look after his business affairs, but his name was still on the list of refugees not permitted to reenter France. Adrienne, who knew far more about such matters and had greater experience in dealing with them, held a legitimate passport and could have crossed the border without trouble, but she was not yet well enough to travel. Business had to wait.

Both of the Lafayettes sent letters to Diane de Simiane, inviting her to visit Lemkuhlen, and she was eager to make the journey at the first opportunity. More than six years had passed since she and Lafayette had last met, but they had not lost interest in each other and both wanted to resume their affair. Adrienne's ailments barred her from sleeping with her husband, so she, too, regarded it as right and natural that Lafayette should return to the arms of his mistress.

There was wild excitement at the château early in February 1798, when word was received that George Washington Lafayette soon would rejoin his family. He had left the United States as soon as he had heard that his parents had been freed from Olmütz, and he was stopping briefly in Paris en route to Hamburg. Already a diplomat, the young man paid a courtesy call on General Bonaparte. Napoleon was out of the city, but he was graciously received by the General's wife, who made a number of flattering remarks about George's father. These comments encouraged Lafayette to believe that the General in Chief, as Bonaparte now called himself, intended to give him a major military command. He did not yet know that flattery was Josephine Beauharnais Bonaparte's stock in trade.

George reached Lemkuhlen in mid-February. He was even taller than his father, a solemn young man with a quick mind, a serious scholar who nevertheless knew how to handle a horse and a sword. President Washington, writing from Mount Vernon, praised him extravagantly. Adrienne said that her son's presence was the best of medicines, and the only fault Lafayette could find with George was that he walked with a slight stoop.

At about the time George was reunited with his parents, the family learned that twenty-year-old Anastasie had fallen in love. Charles de La Tour Maubourg, the younger brother of Lafayette's senior aide, also lived at Lemkuhlen, and the fact that he was penniless, like so many aristocratic French refugees, did not bother him or Anastasie. They had the good sense, however, to wait for an improvement in Charles's prospects before asking Lafayette's permission to marry.

A few weeks after George's arrival Diane de Simiane came to Hamburg. Still radiantly beautiful in her late thirties in spite of the trials she had undergone, she displayed the true delicacy of a French aristocrat by making her home with Mme de Tesse at Witmold. Now Lafayette had a destination when he set out on his daily canters, and Diane also came frequently to Lemkuhlen to see her good friend Adrienne.

Anastasie and Charles finally summoned the courage to ask Lafayette for permission to marry, and he was pleased to give his consent. Adrienne, who had kept her daughter's suitor under close observation, also was delighted, even though Charles's only income came from his older brother. She would have preferred that the young couple wait until the bulk of the La Tour Maubourg fortunes were restored, but that might take years, and in spite of their early resolve, Anastasie and Charles now wanted to be married as soon as possible.

By April 1798 it dawned on Lafayette that his own situation had not improved and that no major changes were imminent.

Perhaps the prospect of having a son-in-law to feed, along with the others for whom he was responsible, caused him to reassess his future. There was no lack of funds, because many people were willing to lend Adrienne as much as she wanted. Her own inheritance from her mother was not yet settled in France, but Foreign Minister Talleyrand, the former bishop, wrote that stability was returning gradually and that she and her sisters ultimately would come into their own.

Lafayette, displaying signs of his old impatience, was reluctant to wait indefinitely. A new plan formed in his mind. He had not taken possession of the large tract of land that the state of Virginia had given him, and he pondered the idea of going to the United States with his family and establishing a permanent home there. Two or three days each week American visitors to Hamburg called on him, obviously regarding him as one of their own, and he knew the United States was the one country on earth where people of every political persuasion would welcome him without question.

He more or less made up his mind to move, but his wife's fragile health was an inhibiting factor. In May, shortly before Anastasie's marriage, Adrienne suffered a relapse and was forced to retire to her bed. Travel was out of the question for her in the foreseeable future, and Lafayette may have been privately relieved. He still entertained the hope, expressed only to Adrienne and to Diane de Simiane, that a need for his services in a major capacity would arise in France.

He still saw himself as the champion of freedom, and believed that sooner or later the call would come. Obviously he did not know that Napoleon Bonaparte had plans of his own that would conflict with his ambitions.

Lafayette revealed his state of mind on May 9, when Anastasie was married at Witmold. The guests expected the father of the bride to appear in the uniform of a marshal of France when he escorted her to the altar. Instead he wore the newly tailored blue and buff of an American major general.

Former military comrades who were now members of Bonaparte's staff wrote frankly to Lafayette that their new commander disliked Lafayette's popularity and was afraid he might become a rival if he returned to France. Lafayette protested that his one desire was to settle down on an estate sufficiently far from Paris to keep him removed from French politics. There he would live the life of a gentleman farmer and would take no part in the nation's affairs.

Certainly this was Adrienne's ambition, which she expressed in numerous letters, but whether her husband really shared it is open to question. In his forty-first year, with his health and vigor completely restored, Gilbert Lafayette was not yet ready to retire. An international hero at nineteen, winner of the Battle of Yorktown and the virtual ruler of France on the eve of the Revolution, he could not bring himself to believe that he had played his last role in history.

He decided to put matters to the test by writing a brief, courteous letter to Bonaparte, offering his services in any capacity in which the General in Chief might find him useful. There was no reply.

Lafayette complained of the snub in a letter to Talleyrand. The diplomat promptly informed him that Bonaparte was no longer in Paris, but was emulating Caesar by leading a large army into Egypt. Lafayette envied him, revealing his own actual feelings by writing to Talleyrand that he wished he could have been a member of the expedition.

By June, Adrienne was feeling sufficiently recovered to think of making a trip to Paris for the sake of straightening out her mother's estate. Her husband agreed that she was better equipped to succeed in such a mission than anyone else, and her sisters concurred. Lafayette was reluctant to allow her to make the journey alone, however. The problem was solved when Virginie volunteered to accompany her mother and take care of her in the event she fell ill again.

In July Adrienne finally left for France, Charles and an already pregnant Anastasie accompanied her as far as the Dutch border. Then she and Virginie went on alone. With the household at Lemkuhlen so depleted, Lafayette gave up his lease on the château and moved back to Witmold with his son.

When Adrienne reached Paris she found the city vastly changed. New parks had been created at the places where guillotines had done their grisly work, shops and cafés had blossomed everywhere, a new middle class was growing wealthy, the poor were as impoverished as ever, and no one talked about the days of the Terror.

Everywhere Adrienne went she was received as a heroine, and even officials of the Directory were excessively polite to her. She had to fight her way through mazes of red tape, Republican bureaucrats having replaced the crown officials who had performed the same functions. So she remained in the city for more than six months, her task complicated by developments at Witmold.

Mme de Tesse had decided to sell her estate because she was afraid of a French invasion, so Lafayette, who had nothing to occupy his time, was being dispossessed. He wrote to his wife urging her to obtain the Directory's permission for him to move to Holland. The Dutch, who regarded him as a great man and were eager to grant him sanctuary, nevertheless were allies of France, and protocol required that they obtain the approval of Paris before such a move was made.

Lafayette had valid surface reasons for wanting to make his

next home in Holland. Anastasie and Charles were already there, having rented a large house outside the little town of Vianen, and it made sense for the entire family to gather there. Among her other tasks in Paris Adrienne was trying to have the La Tour Maubourg brothers removed from the proscribed list, a slow process at best; until the necessary permission was granted, the young people would continue to be supported by Lafayette and his wife. Another reason was that circumstances might make it necessary for Lafayette to go to the United States, and he wanted his wife to live with their children, who could look after her in the event her health deteriorated again.

His most compelling motive, however, emerged in a single sentence in a letter he wrote to Adrienne. "At Vianen," he said, "I will be closer to France than I am at present." His wife, knowing him as she did, must have realized that his continuing exile was growing irksome and that he had no intention of remaining idle indefinitely.

Adrienne quietly added the new burden to her assignments. Contrary to her own fears and those of her family, she was enjoying far better health, and it appeared that activity rather than rest was what she needed. Members of the Directory assured her privately that they would not object if Lafayette wanted to live in Holland. They preferred not to send formal notification to the Dutch government, however, and instead sent an unofficial communication.

It occurred to Lafayette as well as to his wife that their position was stronger than they had realized. Many thousands of Frenchmen continued to admire him, and if the present less than stable government persecuted him, it would become even more unpopular with the people. Lafayette was not so helpless as he had imagined, and he concluded that his view of his situation had been warped because he had been out of touch with realities in rural Holstein.

Adrienne and Virginie arrived at Vianen early in February, and were told that Lafayette, already on the road, was expected at any time. A letter he had written to Anastasie and Charles indicated his conviction that his first grandchild would be a boy. Delayed by floods that made rivers impassable, he and George arrived shortly after Anastasie gave birth to twin daughters. Only one of the infants survived, and she was named Célestine.

When the excitement of domestic events died down Lafayette paid his first visit to nearby Utrecht, where thousands of citizens appeared in the streets to welcome him. Paying a call on the Dutch garrison commander, an old friend, he saw French troops for the first time in many years. They were wearing the red, white, and blue cockade for which he had been responsible, and he wept at the sight.

Bonaparte's invasion of Egypt was causing serious problems for France. England and Austria had revived their alliance against her, and were being joined by Russia and the Ottoman Empire. Lafayette was eager to return to his country's service, and George wanted a commission, too. But Adrienne, having spent a half year in Paris, told her husband and son they would not be accepted by the present regime. Again Lafayette was compelled to wait.

Adrienne's sisters and their families came to Vianen for Easter, and the news from Paris indicated that the return of the estates of the Duchesse d'Ayen was imminent. Adrienne's share would be an estate known as La Grange, located about thirty miles from Paris, and Lafayette considered it ideal for his purposes. Chavaniac, where his elderly aunt still lived, was too far from the capital. At La Grange he could truly emulate President Washington, living the life of a country gentleman while he awaited his country's call to return to duty.

In May 1799 Adrienne returned to Paris, taking her son and younger daughter with her. Again her sisters deputized her to act on their behalf. George had to have his passport renewed, and when he reached Paris he discovered he could be conscripted. A Lafayette might be a danger to the Directory and General Bonaparte as an officer, but as an enlisted man he would be harmless. Adrienne wrote to her husband, asking for advice, and Lafayette's reply was prompt: If it appeared that George might be drafted, he should not wait, and should enter the army without delay as a volunteer. Nearing his forty-second birthday, the Hero of Two Worlds was frank to say, "I envy George."

The mood of France was changing rapidly, as Adrienne learned, and perhaps the most significant sign of a return to tradition was the revival of religion. Sundays were being observed as holidays, priests loyal to the Vatican openly conducted services, and churches were crowded. Former nobles who had regained possession of their ancestral estates were using their titles again, and many of the still growing middle class were beginning to live in luxury. Above all, pride in Napoleon Bonaparte's achievements and the swelling of the ranks of France's enemies were responsible for a sharp rise in the spirit of patriotism that had been almost nonexistent for decades. Adrienne's voluntary incarceration at Olmütz had made her so popular in her own right that crowds surrounded her carriage whenever she left her lodgings.

Sieyès, who still called himself an abbé, joined the Directory in the summer of 1799, and Adrienne promptly went to see him. He indicated that he was in no way opposed to Lafayette's return, but that he did not believe his colleagues were as yet ready for the possible consequences. Also he hinted, or so it seemed to Adrienne, that he thought Lafayette might be utilized as a possible check to the ambitions of Bonaparte.

In July, George rejoined his father, who was depressed by the approach of his forty-third birthday. Almost two years had passed since his release from prison, but he was still living an indolent life. On August 5 he expressed his innermost thoughts in a letter to his wife:

> . . . I shall go to America only when I have lost all hope of serving my country here. When I see the coalition advancing against France and against the whole of humanity, with the most detestable intentions, when I realize that it is my personal enemies who are at the head of this horrible league, I feel that there is nothing for me to do but range myself on the other side and to fight until we have been destroyed. But that cannot be! The other side bears me almost as much ill will! I see no reason to suppose that it is liberty they wish to defend, and I am fully aware of what those motives are that keep me from my native land.

His patience, for him, was extraordinary. An English army, supported by a Russian column, had landed in Holland, and it was possible that he might be captured at any time. But he gave no thought to his own situation, facing the future with his customary equanimity, even though he might be returned to prison.

In September the forces of France and Holland achieved a surprising victory, and the threat of a successful invasion was eased. For the present, at least, Lafayette was safe.

Adrienne continued to exert unremitting efforts in Paris to regain her inheritance, and in order to save money moved into smaller lodgings. Virginie's tutor kept the girl busy at her studies, and she also took music and drawing lessons. The world might be changing, but her parents' standards were unaltered, and she was being reared as a lady.

Diane de Simiane had returned permanently to Paris, and Adrienne not only saw her frequently but reported to Lafayette regularly on the health and spirits of his mistress. Virginie also visited Mme de Simiane.

The allies stepped up their war effort against France, and by October Lafayette was certain he would be recalled at any moment. Still mindful of his honor, he began to lay down conditions in letters to various friends. He would return and help France in her hour of need only if all honorable men were permitted to serve her again, whether they were former nobles or Republicans who had been discredited in the factional disputes that had raged since the early days of the Revolution. It did not cross his mind that he was in no position to make demands.

Early in October General Bonaparte arrived unexpectedly in France, leaving his army behind him in Egypt. Thinking people, Adrienne among them, thought it likely that he soon would make an effort to consolidate all power in his own hands. He conferred with Sieyès when he reached Paris, then retired to his own house, where everyone of consequence visited him. One of the first to call was Adrienne Lafayette, who was accompanied by her daughter.

One facet of Napoleon's genius was his ability to judge character, and he quickly realized Adrienne was an extraordinary woman. Ordering an aide to dismiss others who were waiting to see him, he talked with her for more than two hours. Little of their conversation is known, but apparently he sought her opinions of the current domestic situation.

Adrienne, who was impressed by Bonaparte, repeated one significant comment when she wrote to Lafayette. "Your husband's life," he had said, "is bound up with the preservation of the Republic."

Lafayette's mind seethed. He was prepared to serve his country if she needed him, but he much preferred to lead the simple life of a farmer, he claimed. Perhaps Bonaparte wanted him to come to Paris incognito for a private conference? If so, he was ready to depart at once, and if they hit it off, he would remain; otherwise he would return to Holland.

At Adrienne's insistence he wrote a very short letter to Bonaparte:

Citizen General, it would have been enough for me to love liberty and my country to be filled with joy and hope by the news of your arrival. But to this longing for the common weal I join a deep and lively feeling for my liberator. She whose life I owe to you has told me of the welcome you accorded to the prisoners of Olmütz. I rejoice in the thought of all my obligations to you, Citizen General, and in the happy conviction that to acclaim your glory and to hope for your success is as much a civic duty as it is the expression of personal attachment and gratitude.

Such flattery of a man Lafayette regarded as a colleague was alien to his nature, and is one of a very few letters of this sort that he wrote in his entire lifetime. He sent it only because his wife deemed it wise, and she was the one person, other than his American friends, whose advice he trusted. It becomes obvious that he was prepared to go to almost any lengths in order to gain permission to return to France.

On November 9, after making careful preparations, Napoleon Bonaparte took matters into his own hands. Acting swiftly and aided by Sieyès and his own brother, Lucien, he staged a coup that toppled the Directory. In its place he established a new ruling triumvirate, with himself as first consul. His fellow consuls were Sieyès and a nonentity named Roger-Duclos.

There were no riots, no significant protests of any kind. The people of France were tired of weak governments whose members fought and quibbled with each other; they wanted a strong man to guide the nation, and the strongest in her history took command.

It is impossible to do justice to the complexities of Napoleon Bonaparte's extraordinary character in these pages. He became a dictator who ruled benevolently, granting his subjects all of the personal liberties cherished by Lafayette save one, the right to criticize him. He was responsible for the legal code utilized in France down to the present day, and he encouraged the development of the arts as no man before him had ever done. Perhaps the greatest military mind the world has ever known, he conquered most of Europe, but bled France in the process, driving her to the brink of bankruptcy.

Among his many talents was his uncanny ability to say the right thing at the right time to the right people. His promises to France regarding the restoration of human rights and freedom when he took the helm could have been spoken in all sincerity by Gilbert Lafayette. When he wished, Napoleon could be all things to all men.

Lafayette was elated when the news reached Utrecht. The Directory had disgusted him, and at last a man who saw life as he did was in command. Isolated in a rural Dutch farmhouse and totally out of touch with the world of political affairs, Lafayette felt certain that First Consul Bonaparte intended to place him in charge of the National Guard. What he failed to realize, in his innocence, was that Napoleon, not yet having consolidated his own position, would not be foolish enough to share power with a potential rival.

Adrienne, as usual, understood the situation. For the moment liberty again was the nation's watchword, and if her husband truly intended to return to France instead of just talking about it, now was the precise moment for him to come. Bonaparte, she reasoned, wouldn't want to antagonize France's liberals by expelling Lafayette or sending him to prison. Sieyès was a friend. Roger-Duclos was a nobody, and it didn't matter what he thought or might want.

Acting with extraordinary speed, Adrienne obtained a passport for her husband under a false name. The source of this document has long been a mystery. Foreign Minister Talleyrand may have issued it, wanting to place a check of some sort on the new first consul. The head of the national police, Joseph Fouché, who was another of Lafayette's old friends, may have made out the passport for obscure, convoluted reasons of his own. It is also possible that Adrienne paid a large bribe to some official, although she denied it.

On November 15 an old friend arrived from Paris after a forced ride, bringing Lafayette the passport and a succinct letter from Adrienne. If he intended to return to France, she said, he must make his move instantly.

"It did not take me two minutes to see what I had to do," Lafayette later said. He packed only what he could carry in a saddlebag, said goodbye to Anastasie and Charles, and made a brief speech to his infant granddaughter, assuring the child —who was of course incapable of understanding a word—that they would be reunited in Paris.

Within a few hours of his receipt of his wife's message, the forty-three-year-old General Gilbert Lafayette was on his way back to the France he had not seen in seven years. He would have been on the road even sooner had there not been a last-minute delay. George, who was accompanying his father, was horrified when Lafayette, supposedly traveling incognito, appeared in the full-dress uniform of a marshal of the National Guard. The Dutch would not permit him to leave Holland if he approached the border in uniform, and the French frontier guards would be compelled to arrest him. With great reluctance Lafayette changed back into civilian clothes.

It was not by accident, however, that the horse he rode on the journey was white.

11

Dressed in civilian clothes and traveling without an entourage, Lafayette rode unrecognized through the streets of Paris as he arrived to join his wife. It was just as well, inasmuch as he had no legal right to return to France, but he must have been disappointed that no one knew him. Seven years earlier he had been followed everywhere by large crowds.

Taking the advice of Adrienne and various friends, he made his first move by writing to Bonaparte and to Sieyès. In these identical letters he displayed his customary bluntness and lack of tact:

> Citizen Consul—Since the days when the prisoners of Olmütz owed their liberty to you until now, when the liberty of my country is about to impose upon me even greater obligations to you, I have been thinking that any further extension of my exile can be beneficial neither to the government nor to me. I have this day arrived in Paris.
>
> I am about to leave for a remote part of the country where I shall be united with my family. Before doing so, however,

before even seeing my friends, I have not delayed a moment in addressing myself to you, not that I doubt my place to be wherever the Republic rests upon worthy foundations, but because it is not only my duty but my wish to tell in person of my gratitude.

Sieyès was pleased by the unexpected development. He saw in Lafayette a weapon to prevent Bonaparte from seizing complete power and dismissing the other consuls. Certainly the Abbé was right in thinking that no one other than Lafayette had enough influence with the public to check the ambitions of the First Consul.

Predictably, Bonaparte was furious.

The following day Talleyrand asked Lafayette to call on him, and urged him to return without delay to Holland. Bonaparte was threatening to send him to prison for daring to return to France without permission, and not even good friends had the power to intervene.

Lafayette was prepared to make his own moves in the chess game. He wanted his friends to do nothing for him, he said, because he had no desire to cause troubles for them. If Bonaparte wanted to arrest him, he would make the task easy. He would be glad to surrender himself to the National Guard.

This was reported to Bonaparte, who understood what was at stake. If he ordered the arrest of the man who had founded the National Guard and was still a symbol of liberty to the country, his own claim that he intended to restore the principles of the constitution of 1789 would be seen as a sham. Lafayette had placed him in a delicate position, but he had the power to do as he pleased, and he was subtle enough to get what he wanted if he made the right moves. He understood the character of his potential antagonist; he knew that if he forced a direct confrontation, Lafayette would become stubborn and create a major issue out of the affair. Perhaps he should find some other way.

The Hero of Two Worlds waited restlessly for developments, and forty-eight hours after his return he sent his wife to see the First Consul. Apparently Bonaparte felt a genuine respect for Adrienne Lafayette. He received her with a great show of cordiality, even though he told her in the course of their conversation that she had no understanding of politics.

In this he was mistaken, and undoubtedly he knew it. Adrienne was endowed with a subtlety that matched Bonaparte's. She indicated that her husband was very reluctant to return to idle exile when his country was in danger, and she left the next move to the First Consul.

Bonaparte became oblique, too. Giving no orders and making no threats, he agreed that Lafayette could remain in France without being forced to submit a formal petition for the purpose, and he indicated somewhat vaguely that steps would be taken to end his proscription. It was obvious that he continued to hold the whip hand; Lafayette's name could remain on the list of the banned, ignored for now but there to be discovered if he should step out of line. For the present, then, Bonaparte advised that the returned champion of liberty reside elsewhere than in Paris, where he might be tempted to play an active political role and thus jeopardize his chances of clearing his name.

Bonaparte and Adrienne understood each other. Lafayette was being allowed to remain in France on an informal basis provided he did not interfere in affairs of state.

Adrienne's next step was equally delicate. If her husband believed Bonaparte was issuing orders to him, he would dig in his heels, regardless of the consequences. So she had to convince Lafayette that Bonaparte had merely made a suggestion for the sake of the country's good, and she stressed that she felt the same way.

She had already been awarded a portion of her inheritance, a château at Fontenay-en-Brie, a short distance from La Grange, which would be returned to her in the immediate future. So she proposed that the family go there without delay. Lafayette, as usual, interjected a condition. Since he himself was being allowed to remain in France without being persecuted, there was no reason his elder daughter, son-in-law, and grandchild had to remain in exile.

Adrienne made the arrangements for the termination of the exile of Anastasie and Charles. But she was so afraid her husband might say or do something to create difficulties for himself that she insisted they leave Paris without delay. Only Virginie stayed behind in the city to await her sister.

It must have been a relief to Adrienne when they reached Fontenay without incident. She wrote to the elderly Charlotte de Chavaniac that her husband was "taking no interest in public affairs," and was intending to devote himself exclusively to his family.

Lafayette also wrote to his aunt, saying he hoped to see her in the near future and adding the significant statement:

. . . I have turned my back on politics. The idea of staying longer in Paris, stained as it is with the blood of my relatives and friends, was intolerable to me. I could not be induced to go back there except from a sense of patriotic duty, of which there can be no question since the Revolution is about to be terminated by a power with which I am not associated but which has at its disposal all the means necessary to the doing of much good. . . . I hope that my return will make as little sensation as possible, though without compelling me to resort to concealment. You would do well to address my letters to my wife.

Financial difficulties plagued the reunited Lafayette family at Fontenay and later at La Grange, to which they moved within a few months. Lafayette was in debt to the tune of a quarter of a million livres, and La Grange, when the farm was made operative again, could bring in no more than an estimated 20,000 livres per year. His best hope of putting his affairs in order was to obtain compensation from the government for his extensive properties in Brittany, which had been seized and sold early in the Revolution. He also wanted payment for his properties in Cayenne, which the government also had taken and still held.

Repairs at Fontenay and the restoration of La Grange, not to mention the purchase of furniture for both places, would cost another fortune, but Lafayette and his wife were not deterred by the lack of funds. They hired workmen and landscape gardeners, bought what they required on credit, and in general plunged into these projects as though the Revolution had never taken place.

La Grange was an enormous castle, complete with twin turrets, a moat, a large park, and hundreds of acres of farmland. Lafayette left the selection of furniture to his wife and daughters, and concerned himself with acquiring wheat and rye seed, American corn and tobacco, and cattle, sheep, and pigs. If he was going to live as a farmer, he intended to devote all his energies to his new vocation, and he showed his usual boundless enthusiasm for what lay ahead.

His name remained on the proscribed list, and he agitated constantly to have it removed. He could do nothing for himself, however, so his wife was required to make frequent trips to Paris for the purpose of going from one government bureau to another. She also tried to obtain a military commission for George, which should have been a simple matter, but the new generals, totally loyal to the First Consul, were allergic to the name Lafayette.

Late in 1799 Bonaparte reorganized the consulate, retiring Sieyès on a large pension. For all practical purposes Bonaparte became France's sole ruler, and a new constitution that came into effect before the end of the year merely emphasized that he alone was the government.

Lafayette behaved with unaccustomed discretion during this period. He still felt that as soon as his name was taken from the proscribed list he would be given a position worthy of his reputation, and in letters to his aunt and others he frequently spoke of paying a visit to Bonaparte after the formalities that would give him full citizenship were observed.

In the United States former President Washington died at Mount Vernon on December 14, 1799, and when the news reached Paris a month later Bonaparte immediately ordered that a memorial service be held at the Invalides. Lafayette, deeply disturbed by the passing of his mentor, assumed he would be asked to deliver the principal address. He was not even invited to the ceremonies.

His son attended as the family's representative, standing in line and sitting in the small section to which the general public was admitted. Someone recognized the young man, whose presence was duly reported to Bonaparte, and word came back to Lafayette that the First Consul was annoyed. Even the most determined of optimists must have realized it would be a waste of money to order a new set of uniforms.

It was no easy task for a man accustomed to glory since his teens to live in obscurity, dependent on the favors of an upstart who had gathered the reins of power into his own hands. But Lafayette demonstrated both tact and patience, perhaps for the first time in his life. If Bonaparte was testing him, he met that test. Various friends urged him to go to Paris and rally the liberals in order to prevent the rise of a new dictatorship. He stayed in the country, made no mention of politics in his correspondence, and evoted himself to spending large sums of borrowed money putting La Grange in order. The proprietorship of a model farm was more important to him than the fate of France, or so it seemed.

Early in March 1800 he received the first indications of a thaw. The First Consul, in several conversations, spoke with warmth of Lafayette's patriotism. Paris buzzed, and Lafayette received a number of letters telling him about these comments. A few days later George Washington Lafayette received a commission as a junior lieutenant in the cavalry and was called to active duty on the Italian front, where new fighting was imminent.

Late in March the name of General Gilbert Lafayette unexpectedly appeared on a list of those to whom full citizenship had been restored. No restrictions were placed on his activities, he was entitled to live where he pleased, and he would be allowed to travel abroad. The First Consul had consolidated his position, and no longer was afraid of a potential rival.

Lafayette immediately sent a letter of thanks in which he asked when he could come to Paris to express his gratitude in person. He still expected to be offered a major military command. Instead, he was ignored, Bonaparte going off to rejoin his army in Italy without bothering to reply. Lafayette seems not to have realized that whatever influence he might have exerted was being neutralized by a policy of deliberate neglect.

On June 14 Bonaparte won what may have been his greatest

victory up to that time, the Battle of Marengo, and the Austrians were forced to sue for peace. Lieutenant George Lafayette fought with distinction, and won two commendations.

Even Lafayette's enemies could not deny he was a patriot. The First Consul had snubbed him repeatedly, but the victory at Marengo so delighted him that he sent Bonaparte a warm letter of congratulations.

Returning to Paris in triumph, Bonaparte was now so secure that he felt threatened by no one, and he invited Lafayette to the Tuileries. The two men met for the first time early in July, in the presence of many officials, and Lafayette was unexpectedly impressed. Later he remarked that he recognized genius, feeling as he had when he had first been presented to Frederick the Great. Bonaparte, in turn, went out of his way to be complimentary, saying that the officer the Austrians still feared the most was Lafayette.

A few days later, after his return to La Grange, Lafayette received a visit from an unofficial emissary who informed him that the First Consul would have no objection if he sought a seat in the new Senate. Lafayette had not been completely taken in by flattery, however, and was not prepared to let the new regime take advantage of his name until he saw for himself whether the personal freedoms of individuals would be respected. He didn't necessarily doubt that the First Consul's intentions were good, but a growing maturity caused him to withhold his endorsement until Bonaparte proved himself.

Diane de Simiane paid her first visit to La Grange, having just reestablished her own residence in Paris, and received a warm welcome from her host and hostess. She spent a week with the family, and Lafayette accompanied her to Paris, where he remained with her for several days before going off to Auvergne.

He had two reasons for making the trip: He wanted to see his aunt after so many years of separation, and he felt it was his duty to express his gratitude in person to the many people who had been kind to Adrienne during the worst days of the Revolution.

Auvergne greeted Lafayette with enthusiasm. Entire towns turned out to honor him. The size and enthusiasm of these receptions were duly reported to Bonaparte. On his first evening in Clermont, Lafayette remarked that he would not hesitate to chastise anyone who had been disrespectful to his wife, and the zealous revolutionaries who had made life miserable for Adrienne promptly decided that reasons of health made it essential for them to take themselves elsewhere.

Lafayette spent more than a month with his aunt at Chavaniac, and realized her health was failing. For her sake he busied himself with the restoration of the property, trying to make it look as it had in the days before the Revolution. He received members of the petty aristocracy, priests, old friends of the middle class, and peasants who were still fiercely loyal to him.

His undiminished popularity in the area caused Bonaparte to revise his opinions. The people of Auvergne would have followed the former Marquis de Lafayette wherever he cared to lead them, and the First Consul came to the conclusion that the Hero of Two Worlds might not be harmless after all.

Adrienne Lafayette took advantage of her husband's absence from La Grange to visit Brittany. Experience had made her one of the most clever, hardheaded businesswomen in France, and she not only succeeded in regaining possession of two large properties that had belonged to her husband but collected some substantial debts owed to him. She assigned the properties to her daughters, thereby assuring their future financial stability, and she paid off most of Lafayette's debts. She returned to La Grange with enough cash in hand to loan several thousand livres to Diane de Simiane, who was having trouble claiming her own inheritance.

Relations between France and the United States had deteriorated badly in recent years, bringing the two nations to the verge of an undeclared war, but their friendship was on the mend again, and in October 1800 an American mission came to Paris for a frank discussion of outstanding problems. Lafayette was the first to be invited to see old friends, and went at once to the city.

General Bonaparte deemed it wise to hold a reception for the Americans, and asked Lafayette to attend. Lafayette, impressed anew by Bonaparte's genius, told him in detail that he alone could guarantee the liberties for which so many Frenchmen had died.

The following week, after his return to La Grange, a summons from Talleyrand brought him back to Paris. The First Consul, Talleyrand informed him, was pleased to offer him the post of French minister to the United States. The position would have been a natural, but Lafayette refused, saying he regarded himself as much an American as a French citizen, and that he could not act as the envoy of any foreign nation to the United States.

Apparently Talleyrand was not surprised, and urged him to seek a seat in the Senate, virtually assuring him that no obstacle would be placed in his path. For the second time Lafayette sidestepped, claiming his work on his farm kept him too busy to allow him to do anything else of substance.

By this time Lafayette's views had solidified, and he knew where he stood. He had been heartened by his reception in Auvergne. Scores of old friends, acquaintances, and subordinates called on him whenever he went to Paris, and La Grange was seldom free of visitors. He urged other returned nobles to offer their services to the regime, but his own situation was different. He was a symbol of liberty, as he had been for so many years, and he had no intention of giving a formal stamp of approval to the new regime until he knew where the First Consul really stood.

Bonaparte did not appreciate snubs, particularly when he went out of his way to woo someone who could be useful to him. He let it be known that he was annoyed, but took care not to retaliate. A policy of benign neglect had rendered Lafayette impotent after he had first come back to France, and a return to that approach would be equally effective now.

Lafayette seemed content with the role he had chosen for himself, and his supervision of La Grange kept him busy. There were other diversions. Anastasie gave birth to another daughter, whom she and Charles named Louise. George suffered a slight wound in battle, which delighted his father, who could now claim that a Lafayette of yet another generation was a true soldier. The time had come to think of finding an appropriate husband for Virginie, and many family discussions were held. Diane de Simiane participated in some of these talks, and so did the Comtesse de Tesse, who had returned from exile.

Adrienne's father, known as the Duc de Noailles since the death of his own father, also came back, bringing with him the mistress he had married since the death of his wife. He desperately wanted to be taken off the proscribed list so he could press for the recovery of the properties he had lost during the Revolution. He had no idea how to proceed in either matter, so he turned to the family expert, his eldest surviving daughter. He gave Adrienne no peace, insensitive to the demands her own immediate family made on her time, and nagged her so persistently that he created a domestic crisis.

Lafayette, always the most amiable of men in his dealings with his wife's relatives, had made it his business to get along with them. He had not interfered when she had worked out questions of inheritance with her sisters, and he not only deferred to her in business dealings but relied on her to handle such matters. Under no circumstances would he permit anyone to treat her churlishly, however, and when her father reduced the harried woman to tears he took matters into his own hands.

Making a special trip to Paris for the purpose, he held his first and last confrontation with the Duc de Noailles. Icily polite at first, he quickly lost his temper. After reminding the old man that Adrienne still had not recovered her health, he made it plain he would be forced to sever relations if the Duc de Noailles did not desist and permit Adrienne to deal with the situation in her own manner.

That settled the problem. The startled duke, who long had taken his son-in-law's subservience for granted, not only backed off but wondered whether he might be wise to go back to Switzerland. Adrienne was grateful to her husband, and Virginie noted that the entire family, her aunts and uncles included, now looked at her father with new respect. The sense of obedience to one's elders was so deeply instilled in all members of the family that Lafayette had broken a precedent, and in the eyes of relatives his victory had been as great as any he had ever won on the battlefield.

Late in 1800 Adrienne achieved her greatest business success, an agreement with the government regarding the two plantations in Cayenne that had been taken from her husband. Under terms personally approved by Bonaparte, Lafayette would be given one of the plantations and a cash payment of about 150,000 livres provided he would cede the other property to France. The terms were less than ideal, but the cash payment was sufficiently generous to pay off the debts of the Lafayettes in full and leave them with a substantial sum, so Adrienne accepted. Thanks to her unremitting efforts, the financial crisis was ended.

Two days before Christmas Bonaparte escaped an attempted assassination almost universally believed to have been instigated by the Comte de Provence. Lafayette, who was aware of the chaos that would have ensued had the First Consul been murdered, wrote him a letter of congratulations. His sincerity was so apparent that he was invited to the Tuileries.

There, in the privacy of the First Consul's study, the two men talked for hours, and for the first time established a genuine rapport. An approving Lafayette quoted his host in a letter to Adrienne:

"... You may disapprove of the government, you may think me a despot, but a day will come when they will see whether I have been working for myself or for posterity. But when all is said and done, I am the master of the movement, I, whom the Revolution, whom you, whom all patriots have put where I am, and if I brought back these people [the Bourbons], it would be to hand all over to their vengeance!" These feelings were so nobly expressed and he spoke so well of the glory of France that I took his hand to show how great was the pleasure he had given me.

That was the beginning of a new, unexpected friendship, and Lafayette received frequent invitations to the Tuileries, all of which he accepted. The two men were soldiers who spoke the same language, and they developed a genuine liking for each other. The First Consul had already grown so powerful that few people were willing to tell him anything other than what he wanted to hear, but Lafayette was always blunt, always honest.

What astonished Bonaparte was that Lafayette wanted no favors, no honors, no position for himself. He had established a balance consistent with his own sense of honor, and he sought no change in his status. Presumably he had the tact to refrain from mentioning that he wanted to see in what direction the government was heading before he would commit himself.

Repeatedly Bonaparte asked him, "What can I do for you, General?"

Each time Lafayette replied, "Nothing, General."

That wasn't quite accurate, but it was close enough to the truth. It was a simple matter for Lafayette to request the return of citizenship to his father-in-law and many other nobles who had returned. Bonaparte acquiesced, stipulating only that restoration of citizenship would be limited to those who had not taken up arms against the Republic.

On one occasion the First Consul's sense of social inferiority led him to remark with some bitterness that the returned nobles, in spite of his kindness to them, laughed at him behind his back. Lafayette, according to his own account, replied, "I am astonished that a general who has conquered Europe should condescend to take notice of the grimacings of the Faubourg Saint-Germain."

In April or May 1801 Bonaparte took his new friend into his confidence and told him he hoped to sign an agreement with the Pope that would restore Roman Catholicism to its place as the sole official religion of France.

Lafayette seized the opportunity to preach a doctrine close to his heart, that of religious freedom as guaranteed by the Constitution of the United States. He said, "You had nothing to do with the horrible persecution to which the priests were exposed. You have a clean slate. Take advantage of it to establish the American system. The really pious will bless you—I know their attitude from my own family. All they want is complete freedom for their own form of worship."

Bonaparte replied in equally unvarnished language. "With my political prefects, my police, and my priests, there is nothing I cannot do."

He refrained from mentioning his real goal. In return for the restoration of Catholicism, which would be a triumph for the Vatican, he wanted the Pope to crown him emperor of France.

Lafayette realized what he had in mind, however, and laughed to temper his response. "Confess," he said, "that all this amounts to is that you would like to have the little phial broken over your own head."

"You don't give a damn for the little phial, any more than I do," Bonaparte said. "What matters to us, inside and outside the country, is that the Pope and all his brood should declare against the legitimacy of the Bourbons."

Lafayette and his son spent September and October of 1801 with his aunt at Chavaniac. The old lady wanted to discuss questions of inheritance with him, and he was delighted by her proposal. At her death he would receive a one-quarter share of Chavaniac; it was taken for granted that he, in turn, would leave it to his son. George would be left a one-half interest by his great-aunt, and his sisters would split the remaining quarter. Charlotte de Chavaniac was very fond of George, and the entire visit was amicable. At its conclusion the young officer went off to rejoin his cavalry brigade in Italy.

Diane de Simiane had just recovered her country estate, and with Adrienne's financial help had refurnished it. Lafayette helped her celebrate by stopping off for a two-week visit with her on his way home. Always an attentive husband, he wrote almost daily letters to his wife.

Adrienne had never been busier. Still pursuing the family's business interests, she succeeded, in the autumn of 1801, in winning the restoration of properties belonging to her husband in Touraine. The farms in Brittany were showing a profit, and La Grange was in the black too. Lafayette was able to enjoy his penchant for expansion, and after putting in a new apple orchard he imported more than one hundred head of cattle from England.

After he and Adrienne both returned to La Grange they devoted themselves to a new enterprise, the arrangement of George's marriage to a girl of whom they heartily approved. Emilie de Tracy, with whom George had fallen hopelessly in love, was the daughter of Comte Destutt de Tracy, a distinguished political philosopher who shared Lafayette's enthusiasm for the American experiment in democracy. Tracy, whose wealth and property had been restored and who was able to give his daughter a handsome dowry, was sufficiently realistic to have accepted a seat in Bonaparte's senate.

Adrienne happily began to prepare an apartment for her future daughter-in-law, who came to La Grange for a visit. Anastasie and Virginie participated actively in the planning, and only the master of the house, whose interest in home decoration was limited, was excluded from the project.

He had other matters on his mind. In the late autumn of 1801 Lord Cornwallis took advantage of the state of peace between England and France to pay a visit to Paris, and Lafayette attended a private dinner in his honor. The victor and loser of the Battle of Yorktown were well acquainted by this time, and Lafayette spoke candidly about the restrictions on liberty in France.

His comments were repeated to Bonaparte, as he might have anticipated, and the First Consul was not pleased. The next time Lafayette went to the Tuileries his host said, "I should warn you that, according to Lord Cornwallis, you have not yet seen the error of your ways."

When questions concerning liberty were at stake, Lafayette refused to remain silent or to apologize for his stand. "What errors?" he demanded. "Is it an error to love liberty? What should have turned me against it? The crimes and excesses of the terrorist tyranny? They have merely made me hate still more all forms of arbitrary government, and have strengthened me in my principles."

No one spoke that way to Bonaparte, who was shocked and angry. "I must tell you, General Lafayette," he said, "that I see with regret the manner in which you express your views on the actions of the government. By talking like that you lend the weight of your name to its enemies."

A prudent man would have made his peace with the ruler of France, but Lafayette was never cautious in his defense of freedom. "What else can I do?" he asked. "I live a retired existence in the country. I do my best to avoid talking politics, but whenever anyone asks me whether your regime is in accordance with my ideas of liberty, I am forced to say no. I wish to be a prudent man, General Bonaparte, but not a renegade."

The First Consul glared at him, then stalked from the room.

Had the speaker been anyone but Lafayette, he well might have been arrested or deported. But Bonaparte, always eager to expand his empire, actively sought the support of liberals in many countries, and he knew they would call him a despot if he chastised their hero. In his frustration he could do nothing but refrain from inviting Lafayette to the Tuileries.

Some of Lafayette's friends were concerned for his safety,

but he shrugged off their fears. Adrienne, as always, strongly supported his stand.

Word of the altercation spread through Paris, and Lafayette was recognized as the one man in France who dared to oppose the First Consul. The breach widened, and many months would pass before it would be healed. In the meantime Lafayette refused to absent himself from Paris or take other precautions.

"My opinions are well known," he said, "and I shall not alter them."

12

One facet of Napoleon Bonaparte's genius was his talent for detail. He not only thought in all-encompassing, long-range terms, but studied minutiae that would have been presumed beneath his notice. As a direct result of this propensity, Gilbert Lafayette suddenly discovered, late in 1801, that his deal with the government for his Cayenne properties was in jeopardy. Bonaparte was getting even, in a picayune way, for Lafayette's outspoken defense of liberty.

The situation was embarrassing because the Lafayettes had expected the payment of 150,000 livres to have been made by that time, and they were short of cash. Adrienne went to Paris for innumerable conferences with Talleyrand and other officials, but the red tape became even more snarled.

Early in the spring of 1802 Lafayette took matters into his own inexperienced hands. He knew what needed to be done, and he stormed into various government bureaus, demanding immediate action and threatening to go directly to the First Consul if the matter were not settled. Should a meeting with

Bonaparte fail to resolve the impasse, he would be compelled to tell the whole story to his American friends, and he felt certain they would pass along the tale of government duplicity in a financial agreement to the newspapers of the United States.

The difficulties cleared up overnight, and the agreement was signed by the government on April 3, 1802. Lafayette received an immediate cash payment of 140,000 livres, the largest sum he and his wife had seen in many years.

Perhaps this fortune was responsible for the development of snags in the marriage contract being worked out with the father of Emilie de Tracy. The Senator objected to the terms of old Charlotte de Chavaniac's will; the ancestral estate of the Lafayette family, he said, should be passed intact to George.

Aunt Charlotte had her own ideas in the matter. Under no circumstances would she cut her beloved nephew out of her will, and under no circumstances would she fail to provide for Anastasie and Virginie. The girls had been devoted to her during the Terror, and she insisted on remembering them.

The marriage of George and Emilie was in danger of being canceled, and the bride-to-be was reduced to hysteria. Adrienne solved the problem: She and her husband would pay George the sum of 20,000 livres after Aunt Charlotte died, to compensate him for his sisters' shares in the estate. This satisfied the money-grubbing senator, and the wedding date was set.

The signing of a peace treaty with England was used by Bonaparte to prepare the public for his own ambitious plans. He was hailed in the press as the savior of France, and on Easter Sunday he rode to Nôtre Dame Cathedral in the royal carriage last used by Louis XVI. In the cathedral he sat on a special throne, and was accorded the homage due only a reigning king. In the days that followed, his supporters proposed that a national referendum be taken on the question of whether Bonaparte should be made first consul for life.

A surge of patriotic fervor swept France, and Gilbert Lafayette always was susceptible to such sentiments. He sent Bonaparte a warm letter, congratulating him on the official termination of the war with Great Britain and, above all, on the complete restoration of French national honor.

The First Consul responded in kind, and Lafayette was granted a pension of 6,000 livres a year, the maximum permitted under existing law. This generous gesture signaled the end of their feud, at least for the moment.

On the question of granting Bonaparte his title for life, however, Lafayette had his own ideas. He had suggested a lifetime presidency for George Washington in the United States, and believed France should do the same for Bonaparte, but only on condition that constitutional guarantees were adopted to prevent an abuse of power or the creation of a new hereditary monarchy. He did not proselytize for his view, however; he knew it would have been a waste of time.

The referendum was held. More than 3,500,000 voters favored the granting of a lifetime first consulship, and only some 9,000 were opposed. Lafayette was one of this handful. He not only voted according to his conscience, but made sure his views would be called to the attention of Bonaparte. He wrote on his ballot, "I cannot vote for such an office until such time as public liberty shall have received sufficient guarantees. Then, and then only, will I give my support to Napoleon Bonaparte." And he signed his name. Later in the day he expressed these same views in a long letter to the First Consul, but coupled them with his best personal wishes for success and good fortune.

Lafayette was naive, but even he must have realized that by taking this stand he was terminating all relations with the man who had made himself the ruler of France. Under no circumstances could Bonaparte continue to receive him. All the same, Lafayette had felt compelled to make his views known. He made no attempt to publicize them, and only through the First Consul himself did they become known to a small circle near the top.

Most high officials and those in the ruler's circle believed that Lafayette had lost his reason. Only Bonaparte himself seemed to understand that his conscience had demanded the taking of such a stand, and only Bonaparte appreciated his courage. Now that his own position was secure, Bonaparte could afford to be generous, and although he did not invite Lafayette to the Tuileries again, he often referred to him, giving him his due for the role he had played at the start of the Revolution.

These comments were duly passed along to Lafayette, who accepted them calmly. His whole attitude is worthy of note. He had done the bidding of his conscience, he had no fear of the possible consequences, and he was content. If he lacked diplomacy, his sense of honor was intact, and nothing else mattered to him. "The worst anyone can do to me," he wrote to Thomas Jefferson, now president of the United States, "is kill me, so I have nothing to fear from any man or any power." At forty-five years of age he had become impervious to the feelings that influenced lesser mortals.

Family matters rather than politics occupied the attention of the head of the house of Lafayette in the summer and autumn of 1802. He put in a pear orchard at La Grange, and imported one hundred sheep from Holstein. His father-in-law, although possessing a valid passport, bogged down in his negotiations to recover the Hôtel de Noailles and went back to Switzerland to live.

Emilie de Tracy and George were married in June, and the young couple spent their honeymoon at La Grange. Lafayette established a rapport with his daughter-in-law that persisted for the rest of their lives, and an amused Anastasie observed that "when Emilie smiles, Papa becomes her slave."

Now it was time to think of a marriage for Virginie, whose spirit of independence caused the whole family to liken her to her father. Her aunt Pauline proposed a candidate: Louis de Lasteyrie was tall, exceptionally handsome, and somewhat different than the usual young nobleman. He had been reared in Malta, an uncle who ranked high in the order of the Knights of Malta having taken him there during the worst days of the Revolution, and, like members of the Lafayette family, he entertained reservations about Bonaparte.

Adrienne and her husband met Louis, decided he was a worthy suitor, and invited him to La Grange. Under the traditional system, still followed by the restored nobility, marriages were arranged by families, and the bride and groom were given little choice in the selection of their mates. Many families, however—and the Lafayettes were one—would not insist on a marriage that their children found repugnant. Adrienne and her sisters were afraid Virginie would reject Louis as a suitor, and the young man's uncle had to caution him not to be rude. Both families were pessimistic.

But Virginie and Louis were attracted to each other at first sight, and a scant ten days later the young man formally applied for her hand. Lafayette was not known for his sense of humor, but he couldn't resist teasing the infatuated couple. He called a formal family conference, at which he, Charles, and George questioned Louis at length about his political opinions. Anastasie interrogated Virginie, but Emilie, a bride of only a few months, was too tenderhearted to play the role of inquisitor that had been assigned to her. With mock solemnity Lafayette requested that the entire family vote by secret ballot. To the surprise of no one, Louis was accepted, and Lafayette would have one more mouth to feed.

Paris was full of British visitors in 1802, and the liberal Whigs made pilgrimages to La Grange, where the Lafayettes entertained them in style. Prominent among them was Charles James Fox, who was accompanied by his wife. He shared Lafayette's dedication to the cause of liberty and was openly critical of Bonaparte. The First Consul was not unaware of this attitude, and remarked morosely that La Grange was becoming a center of dissent.

The marriage of Virginie and Louis was planned for the early spring of 1803, but had to be postponed because Lafayette slipped and fell on the ice in a Paris street one day and broke his leg. He was carried to the house of the Comtesse de Tesse, and there a team of physicians waited on him. After examining him they gave him a difficult choice: If he allowed his leg to heal in the usual way, by resting comfortably and subjecting it to no strain, he would be crippled for life; if, on the other hand, he permitted them to put his injured limb in a newly invented device known as a press, which caused excruciating pain, the treatment might effect a complete cure.

Lafayette unhesitatingly chose "the wheel," as he came to call it. His suffering was so great that the women of his family saw to it that he was never alone. Adrienne, Mme de Tesse, Anastasie, and Virginie took turns sitting at his bedside, and they marveled at his stoicism. Not once did he cry out or complain, but his agony was so great that for hours at a time he could not speak.

Talleyrand was a frequent caller, as were the Comte de Bernadotte, later the king of Sweden, and General Thaddeus Kosciuszko, a fellow hero of the American Revolution. Bonaparte made no direct inquiries and sent no emissaries to the house of Mme de Tesse, but privately indicated his concern by demanding that copies of the physicians' reports be sent to him.

After six weeks the device was removed, and Lafayette's relief was so great that tears came to his eyes. He discovered that his leg was stiff, and the painful treatment had not accomplished its purpose. Thereafter he had to walk with the aid of a stick. He detested it and ultimately learned to move without it, but as he grew older the leg troubled him in damp weather, and he was forced to rely on it again. The paintings of him made during middle age and in his later years invariably show him gripping a cane in one hand.

In the spring Lafayette became a grandfather again, Emilie giving birth to a daughter who was named Nathalie. A short time later Virginie and Louis were married, and like the other members of the younger generation they settled at La Grange.

The Treaty of Amiens provided only a short breathing spell, and by 1803 the resumption of war between France and Great Britain became inevitable. Bonaparte would not be satisfied until he dominated the entire Continent, and this the British, fearing isolation, would not permit.

The First Consul needed money for the resumption of hostilities. Realizing that British control of the sea would make it difficult for France to maintain her colonies in the New World, he sold the vast Louisiana Territory to the United States for 80,000,000 livres, or $15,000,000. This vast tract comprised more than 825,000 square miles, and the territory of the United States was increased by 140 percent. Lafayette rejoiced

172

for his second homeland.

Louis de Lasteyrie was unable to obtain a commission in the army, and it may be that he was refused one because he was Lafayette's son-in-law. But George had been recalled to duty, and Louis, determined not to be denied the chance to serve his country, enlisted as a private. He was stationed near Paris, and consequently returned to La Grange for weekends.

Early in 1804 a complex royalist plot against Bonaparte was unearthed, and Lafayette was suspected of being a major participant. Joseph Bonaparte, the First Consul's brother, laughed aloud at the charge, saying he found it inconceivable that Lafayette would connive with Bourbons, who would destroy all personal liberties if the Comte de Provence ever ascended the throne. Bonaparte himself demanded a thorough investigation, however, and it was rumored that Lafayette soon would be arrested and imprisoned.

Members of the American legation heard the stories and forwarded them to their new capital city, Washington. An alarmed President Jefferson wrote to Lafayette and made him a specific proposal. He suggested that Lafayette move without delay to the Louisiana Territory, where he would feel at home because French was the native language there. He would be given a plot of 12,000 acres, as well as a handsome town house in New Orleans, and would have the right to purchase as much additional land as he wished at a very small price. Within a short time he would be wealthier than he had ever been. What was more, Jefferson said, he was held in such high esteem everywhere in the United States that as soon as he became acclimated it was "possible" he would be made governor of the entire Louisiana Territory. More than this no president could offer.

Bonaparte was determined to trace the conspiracy to its

roots, and agents of the national police paid several visits to La Grange, where they questioned Lafayette at length. Many of his friends, who shared the fears of the Americans for his safety, urged him to leave for the United States as soon as possible.

Instead he sent a long letter of regret to Thomas Jefferson. He was grateful for the continuing friendship of the President and the American people, but circumstances made it impossible for him to contemplate such a move. His wife's health was frail, he said, and she was incapable of making such a long and arduous voyage. He himself was lame, and had not yet recovered his full strength. In fact, he found it necessary to rest every few hours. His wife was very reluctant to part with her three granddaughters, who were the joy of her life, and he wouldn't enjoy the wrench, either. His aged aunt, Charlotte de Chavaniac, was now eighty-three years old, and he was afraid his migration to America would kill her.

Finally he came to his real reason for refusing the generous offer. He could not bring himself to leave France while "a chance of liberty" there remained.

Only a perennial optimist could have believed that greater freedom was in store for France. Late in the spring of 1804 Bonaparte organized the establishment of an empire under a hereditary monarchy, and freely gave titles to his relatives, generals, and political supporters. On December 2, having already functioned as emperor for more than six months, he was to be crowned by Pope Pius VII, who had agreed to come to Paris for the ceremony. At the last moment, as the Pope lifted the crown, Napoleon snatched it from his hands and placed it on his own head.

Nobles of the old regime fell all over themselves and each other in their haste to win high-paying positions and honors.

Only the recluse of La Grange remained aloof, and his refusal to bend his knee or seek to feed at the trough annoyed Napoleon, who sometimes referred to him as "my enemy."

But the Emperor found it hard to believe that any man would refuse wealth and increased stature indefinitely. A new campaign was launched to win Lafayette's support for the regime, which would give the empire a greater legitimacy in the eyes of liberals everywhere.

Napoleon had just formed a new order of chivalry, the Legion of Honor. Joseph Bonaparte, who had remained on friendly terms with Lafayette, sounded him out on the possibility of his taking a place as one of the high officers of the Legion. There would be no duties he would be required to perform, no oaths of loyalty to take. Lafayette quietly demurred, saying he would be grateful if no formal offer were made.

Members of the clergy joined in the campaign. Among them were the Bishop of Vannes, an old friend of the family, and several priests, all of whom went to work on the ladies of the family. Adrienne, her daughters, and her daughter-in-law, who attended mass regularly, made the same bland reply. General Lafayette, they declared, made up his own mind in all things, and no member of the family ever tried to influence him. Priests who called on him found him affable but firm, and he refused to discuss politics with them.

In the summer of 1804 Louis de Lasteyrie was promoted to the rank of corporal in the Dragoons, and the family celebrated. It was a considerable achievement for anyone related to Lafayette to win a promotion. By this time George Lafayette was a senior lieutenant, but by the end of the year it became evident that his military career had reached a dead end. Several generals friendly to Lafayette gave his son a place on their staffs at one time or another, then recommended him for promotion to captain, but these requests were never granted. They were not denied, either; they were simply ignored.

It was obvious that the fine hand of Napoleon was at work. If Lafayette could not be bribed, tempted, or persuaded to join him, then George and Louis would be made to suffer, and Lafayette's ambitions for them would be thwarted. Both of the young men were unhappy, but neither dreamed of asking Lafayette to make his peace with the Emperor for their sakes. Principle was far more important at La Grange than promotion.

Lafayette spent 1804 and 1805 quietly, rarely visiting Paris and making no comment on political matters to the many visitors who came to La Grange. He delighted in showing his friends his thriving farm, and spent hours talking about cattle and new strains of wheat, but he became conveniently deaf when the name of Napoleon was mentioned.

He was wise to remain so silent. The annoyed emperor would have liked to deport him, at the very least, but could do nothing as long as Lafayette refrained from expressing a single disloyal word. Napoleon liked to boast that the world was at his feet, but Lafayette stood on his own.

Aside from occasional trips to Auvergne to see Charlotte de Chavaniac, Lafayette stayed at home. In the spring of 1805, while Adrienne was visiting her father in Switzerland, it was rumored that the Emperor had issued an order forbidding the master of La Grange to set foot in Paris. Joseph Bonaparte denied the story, adding with a laugh, "It really wouldn't matter, you know. General Lafayette never comes here anyway."

Three or four times each year Diane de Simiane came to La Grange, usually staying for a month to six weeks. She was still Adrienne's close friend, and all of the younger people called her "aunt." Lafayette continued to confide in her, but whether they still slept together is impossible to determine. When Mme de Simiane wrote, she usually sent her letters to Adrienne or to Virginie, the most indefatigable of the family's correspondents. If Lafayette wrote to her during this period, his letters have been lost.

Napoleon planned to invade England, realized he could not succeed, and instead launched attacks on the combined forces of Austria and Russia. Lafayette's son and son-in-law participated in these 1805 campaigns, and Adrienne worried about them. Lafayette felt certain they would win glory, which they did, but they received no credit for their gallantry, which irritated but did not surprise him. By the end of the year Napoleon had achieved some of his greatest victories, culminating in the Battle of Austerlitz, which forced the dissolution of the coalition against him.

His star was still rising, but Gilbert Lafayette's campaign of silent resistance to tyranny was bearing fruit. In the United States, where he remained newsworthy, people were reminded by politicians that he was faithful to the principles of freedom. In London, where Napoleon was denounced daily in Parliament, the Whigs were quick to point out that Lafayette's silence spoke for vast numbers of French people. In Switzerland, the Low Countries, and Scandinavia large numbers of liberals expressed their admiration for Lafayette. No matter how great Napoleon's achievements, the reproving shadow of the unspeaking ghost fell across him, and Lafayette gave him no excuse for acting.

Lafayette's early biographers wrote that he spent these difficult years in retirement, which is true, but he was more than a gentleman farmer enjoying a bucolic life with his family. He regarded himself as the conscience of France, and it was gratifying to learn that people in many countries appreciated the stand he was taking. Aware of the risks, he walked a tightrope. He acquired wisdom as he matured, and by 1806, when he was only one year short of fifty, he was no longer the flaming man of action. The greater Napoleon's exploits, the stronger grew the symbolic value of Lafayette's silence.

When visitors to La Grange mentioned politics he firmly changed the subject. When asked directly what he thought of the Emperor, he offered his friends grapes from his own vineyards, apples and pears and peaches from his own orchards. If the secret police were opening and reading the mail of suspected dissidents, as was widely rumored, they could find no hint of subversion in Lafayette's letters.

Necessity had made the champion of freedom crafty.

13

Napoleon's battlefield triumphs were dazzling. In the summer of 1806 he dissolved the Holy Roman Empire, and when he gave crowns to his brothers—Joseph was named king of Naples and Louis Bonaparte was awarded the crown of Holland—a new coalition was formed against him by Prussia, Russia, England, and Sweden. Late in 1806 he crushed the Prussians at Jena and defeated the Duke of Brunswick-Lüneburg at Auerstedt, then occupied Berlin, and in 1807 he brought the Russians to their knees at Friedland. The new coalition was smashed. Only Britain still opposed him, and in an effort to mobilize the entire continent against her he invaded Spain and Portugal. Napoleon was brilliant and invincible.

He was also unforgiving in his personal animosities. Corporal Louis de Lasteyrie was promoted to sergeant, but in spite of the leadership he demonstrated in combat he could not win a commission. Lieutenant George Lafayette saved the life of his commander, General Emmanuel de Grouchy, in the Battle of Eylau, in February 1807. The grateful general requested his promotion to captain in a firmly worded letter. The Emperor personally rejected the recommendation.

George and Louis finally realized they had no real future in Napoleon's army, and both wrote that they intended to retire to civilian life as soon as they could be mustered out. Louis was particularly anxious to come home because Virginie was pregnant.

Not even Napoleon's great victories caused Lafayette to break his silence. He sent the Emperor no congratulations, and when Talleyrand, who paid a visit to La Grange, asked him what he thought of the conquests, he replied in a single sentence worthy of a diplomat. "I am a Frenchman," he said, "therefore I rejoice." Even Pauline de Montagu, who had been so critical of her brother-in-law's attitudes after his release from Olmütz, now admired him without reservation.

On April 7, 1807, the clan gathered at La Grange for a celebration of Gilbert and Adrienne Lafayette's thirty-third wedding anniversary. Only the two young soldiers were missing. Even within the confines of the family circle Lafayette refused to comment on Napoleon. When Rosalie de Grammont asked him to say something appropriate to the times, he toasted his wife. Adrienne was forced to retire early, which put something of a damper on the party. She was suffering from the severe headaches that had plagued her when she left Olmütz, and her husband was increasingly concerned about her health.

In June, Virginie gave birth to her first child, a daughter whom she named Pauline. Lafayette wondered aloud if he would live long enough to see the arrival in the world of his first grandson. In August a matured and embittered George came home, much to the delight of his wife and his mother, and resigned his commission. Following the example of his father, he gave no reasons, made no charges against anyone, and gave the Emperor no excuse to arrest any member of the Lafayette family for disloyalty.

Late in September 1807, while Lafayette was on a visit to Chavaniac, his wife fell ill. A Paris physician went out to La Grange to see her and prescribed medication that did her no good. Two weeks later she was moved to the house of the Comtesse de Tesse in the city because it was easier to treat her there. Anastasie wrote to her father, and he came at once to Paris.

His presence cheered her, and she seemed to improve. Her attitude was optimistic, and she told Diane de Simiane that she was suffering from a malignant fever, but would recover. Her condition continued to deteriorate, however, and by December her mind began to wander.

Lafayette stayed at her bedside throughout her illness, refusing to leave her room and sleeping on a couch in a corner. Other members of the family helped him, but he insisted on nursing her himself.

Louis de Lasteyrie arrived home, having been granted his discharge from the army, and went at once to see his mother-in-law. At first she did not know him, and at their next meeting she had forgotten that he and Virginie were married. On December 24 she became lucid and calmly remarked, "Today I am going to see my mother."

Her husband and children were at her bedside when she died that night at the age of forty-eight.

The funeral was held at La Grange, where she was buried, and Lafayette's grief was so great that he collapsed. For a week it was feared that he would follow Adrienne, but he gradually recovered his strength and equilibrium.

His attachment to Adrienne's memory, however, was intense and morbid. For the rest of his life he carried on his person a fragment of a poem she had written. Her bedroom was left as it had been in her lifetime, and Lafayette had the room sealed. Workmen were called in to build a secret entrance to the room, and he went there frequently to meditate. His daughters believed that he prayed, too, but refrained from mentioning the matter to him. Each year, on the anniversary of Adrienne's death, he went to her bedroom and remained there for at least twelve hours. No one knew what he did during this vigil, and no one dared to ask him.

During his illness and convalescence George took charge of affairs at La Grange, but by the spring of 1808 Lafayette was able to become active again. The farm was his mainstay, and he spent the better part of each day in the fields, even though his stiff leg ached when he spent too much time on it. He rode with difficulty, however, and had to give up his daily canter.

With Adrienne no longer at hand to restrain him, Lafayette became more candid in his correspondence, and was unwavering in his defense of freedom. He continued to disapprove of the Empire, and his opinions were duly reported to Napoleon.

"The whole world has become readjusted, with the single exception of Lafayette," the Emperor said. "He has not retreated an inch. He may seem quiet and peaceful enough, but mark my words, he is capable of starting all over again."

Gradually Lafayette formed a new way of life. He slept for about seven hours each night, then attended to his correspondence for another two hours before leaving his bed. His long inspection of the farm was thorough, and dinner was not served until sundown.

George and Emilie were permanent residents at La Grange. Anastasie and Charles moved to a house of their own not far from the farm, and Virginie and Louis also purchased a small property nearby. Lafayette's daughters visited him daily, and did what they could to help Emilie curb his appetite. He had always eaten moderately, but after Adrienne's death he began to consume enormous meals, and for the first time in his life he became overweight. A lack of physical exercise also contributed to his corpulence. Three or four years passed before he made a conscious effort to reduce his girth.

Late in 1808 Virginie gave birth to a boy, who was duly named Gilbert. Lafayette filled La Grange with guests in honor of his first grandson. The boy became his favorite, and soon Virginie was complaining that "Papa has cast aside all disciplines."

In 1809, after Lafayette's year of mourning ended, he resumed his relationship with Diane de Simiane. Occasionally he went to her home in Paris, or to her house in the country, but he disliked leaving his farm for more than a few days at a time, so it was more convenient for her to come to La Grange. Late in 1809 a private suite was established for her, and soon she was spending the better part of each year there. Lafayette's children and their spouses accepted her presence as normal and natural, and when she was in residence Mme de Simiane behaved like the mistress of the house rather than a guest.

She and Lafayette could have married, had they wished, but apparently the idea did not occur to either of them. They had established a pattern three decades earlier, and perhaps they continued to follow it out of habit. It is possible, of course, that his morbid attachment to the memory of his wife may have stood in the way.

Mme de Tesse followed her niece in death in 1810, and in the following year Charlotte de Chavaniac died. Lafayette's circle was growing smaller, and he grieved deeply for his aunt.

Napoleon's continuing successes left him unmoved. He expressed himself with his customary candor in a letter to Thomas Jefferson on April 3, 1809:

> The roads to Paris are covered with kings and princes who come to pay their court. . . . I had rather they were popular deputies to a general federation of liberty and equality, but I cannot help observing what has been the prodigious influence of that revolutionary movement although misguided on its way, and the enthusiasm and talents of which an aristocratic monarchy should ever have prevented the display.
>
> In order to satisfy this mania, geographically gigantic and morally petty, we have had to waste an immense intellectual and physical force, apply a Machiavellian genius to degrade liberal and patriotic ideas, to debase parties, opinions and peoples, unite the glory of a brilliant administration to the foolishness, taxes and vexations necessary to a despotic system, remain suspicious of independence and industry, hostile to light, opposed to the natural advance of the century. Napoleon's existence has had to be founded on nothing but the maintenance of success.

By his fifty-second year Lafayette had become something of a philosopher, and if his own principles had remained unchanged, he could at last see that glory for its own sake was meaningless. His dilemma was cruel: He was saddened by Napoleon's excesses at the expense of liberty, but as a Frenchman he found it difficult to wish for the downfall of France. Perhaps he could have taken an active role in opposition to the Emperor, but his high sense of patriotism made it impossible for him to contemplate such action. He maintained his policy of remaining silent in public, but now he did permit himself to say what he pleased in private.

By 1810 Napoleon effectively expanded his influence to most of Europe. He had created what he himself called "the greatest empire in history," and his power was at its height. In July of that year Lafayette wrote again to Jefferson:

> The recital of the acts of imperial power, singular mixture of greatness borrowed from the revolution and counterrevolutionary abasement, will tell you of our triumphs over foreign enemies, the recent aggrandizement of our territory beyond the limits suited to us, as well as the new measures against public liberty.

There was nothing he could do to curb Napoleon, nothing that any Frenchman could do, but he did not despair. Sitting in front of the fire of the great hall at La Grange after dinner, surrounded by his still-increasing family, he counseled patience. "A study of political movements through the centuries," he told George one night, "convinces me there is a natural pendulum in the affairs of men. The insanity of today will be followed by the sweet reason of tomorrow. If we remain steadfast in holding to our own beliefs, the time will come when men who feel and think as we do will rise up, take the affairs of government into their own hands, and restore liberty to the people of France, who have been promised so much and given so little. The revolution is not dead. For its own protection it must pretend to be asleep."

He was no longer in contact at any time with the Emperor or members of his family. Out of consideration for old friends like Talleyrand and Fouché, both now high-ranking members of the nobility, he refrained from calling on them or corresponding with them, knowing that Napoleon would not appreciate such signs of friendship with a political outcast. He was a pariah by choice, but he did not lose faith, and was convinced that liberty would be restored to the people in his own lifetime.

185

This conviction, perhaps, kept him young in appearance as well as in spirit. In 1811 he and Diane de Simiane had their portraits painted. Even allowing for the artist's possible flattery, both were remarkably youthful. Mme de Simiane, who was fifty, had the face and figure of a thirty-year-old woman, although she had endured her share of suffering. The fifty-four-year-old Lafayette had an unlined face, a clear complexion, and the same direct, intense gaze that every painter had captured since his youth. With the aid of his walking stick he held himself erect, and only his paunch indicated his advancing age.

His weight was still a problem, but there was little he could do to solve it. His leg was stiff, curbing his horseback riding, and he could no longer remain on his feet for hours at a time. George had taken over many of his duties as manager of the farm, and he was increasingly sedentary. "My only consolation when I look at my stomach," he told Virginie in 1811, "is that Napoleon is even heavier."

The Emperor's most ambitious and daring campaign, the invasion of Russia in 1812, marked the beginning of the end of an era. France had been exhausted by Napoleon's wars, satiated by his victories, but the nation responded one last time, and few people realized the extent of his gamble. Lafayette was one of the few.

"At the moment," he said, "immense continental forces under Napoleon are about to attack the Russian Empire, starting from the banks of the Nieman. Will Alexander offer battle? Will he ask for a conference? In both cases he runs the risk of being defeated or caught; but if he chooses to drag out the war, he may well put his rival in an awkward situation."

Tsar Alexander I elected to employ the strategy Lafayette had envisioned, and Napoleon captured Moscow, but was forced to draw back. A combination of guerrilla attacks in strength and the vicious cold of the Russian winter decimated his forces, and he limped back to Paris, with the coalition prepared for the kill.

"We have been bled white," Lafayette wrote Jefferson.

Everyone has lost friends and relatives, every house is in mourning. If Bonaparte had frankly organized ancient Poland and finally granted independence and liberty to all behind him, he might have justified his wars and repaired his earlier conduct; but never did his idea of glory rise above universal monarchy.

The allies gathered themselves for a final blow, and yet another coalition was formed. "Bonaparte may be inadequate as a king because he does not understand the aspirations of the people he rules," Lafayette told Virginie, "but as a soldier he has no equal. I venture to say that this time he will meet his match because he has too few regiments."

The coalition forces attacked in 1813, defeating the Emperor in the Battle of Leipzig. Napoleon fought what many students of military history have regarded as his most brilliant campaign, but not even his genius could prevail against the forces aligned against him. He was forced to retreat into France, and in April 1814 his conquerors compelled him to abdicate. He was sent to the Mediterranean island of Elba in honorable exile.

Lafayette demonstrated sound judgment in an epitaph he sent to Jefferson:

The strong and singular genius of Napoleon had been disharmonized by the folly of his ambition, the unmorality of his mind and this grain of madness not incompatible with great talents, but which is developed by the love and success of despotism. He trifled with and literally lost immense armies, sent abroad

187

all the military stores of France, left the country defenseless, and exhausted and avowed a determination to have the last man, the last shilling of Europe.

As the end drew near, Lafayette stirred from his self-imposed lethargy. He was fifty-seven years old, and had spent the past twenty-two years in political exile. All through the month of March 1814, as the coalition forces drew closer to Paris, he made attempts to rally the forces of liberalism.

But the rigid silence he had maintained worked against him. He was out of touch with men who might have rallied to his cause, and although he was still a symbol, he was indeed a statue without a pedestal. On the last day of March, Russian troops marched into Paris.

14

Talleyrand performed one of his more astonishing feats of political gymnastics when, keeping his post as foreign minister, he negotiated with the victorious allies. The results of those talks were a foregone conclusion. Austria, Russia, and Prussia insisted on the return of the Bourbons to France, and were supported by the Tories in Great Britain. English Whigs and the outnumbered liberals on the Continent countered with the proposal that a constitutional monarchy be established and that Lafayette be made prime minister, but their voices were drowned by the cheers for the departure of Napoleon.

Lafayette was deeply moved by the stirring changes, and spent most of March at Diane de Simiane's town house in Paris. In spite of his dedication to liberty, he had been loyal to Louis XVI, and he fooled himself into believing that the elevation of the Comte de Provence to the throne as Louis XVIII meant that the creation of a constitutional monarchy was near.

On April 12, less than a day after Napoleon's abdication, the Comte d'Artois, the second brother of Louis XVI, arrived in

Paris and took possession of the Tuileries, the new king having been delayed by an attack of gout. One of the first to call on him was Lafayette, who forced himself to wear the white cockade of the Bourbons for the occasion.

Lafayette revealed the reasons for his visit in his *Memoirs:*

> I had more means of seeing the future than most of the others; my associations in youth, my dealings with the princes, my contemporaries, my constant dealings with their parties, everything warned me that this restoration would be but a counterrevolution, more or less openly disguised. I should have been too wary to have recalled the Bourbons myself, but, such is the force of first impressions, I saw them again with pleasure, the sight of the Comte d'Artois in the road moved me greatly, I forgave them their wrongs, even those against my country, and I wished with all my heart that liberty might mix with the reign of the brothers and daughter of Louis XVI.

Lafayette's appearance at the Tuileries created a sensation, and the family and supporters of the new king were delighted. The champion of freedom was making a gesture he had stubbornly withheld from Napoleon, and it was expected that many thousands who were less than enthusiastic over the restoration would follow his lead. Nothing better explains the hopes and fears that warred in his mind than a letter he sent that same month to Jefferson:

> Yet among inexcusable faults and deplorable weaknesses, two evident facts must be acknowledged. There has been a more proper sense and a positive care of public liberty under the Restoration than at the time of Charles II, and there are more symptoms and chances of freedom than could ever have been expected under the masterly despotism and iron hand of Bonaparte. . . . Bonaparte or the Bourbons have been and still are

the alternative in a country where the idea of a republican executive has become synonymous with the excesses committed under that name. In the meanwhile you see the king of Spain, a vile fool, restoring the Inquisition after having expelled the Cortes; the Pope is reestablishing the old system; the king of Sardinia destroying every useful innovation made in the Piedmont, and Austria submitting her ancient possessions to the illiberal system of her Cabinet. Yet the advantages derived from the first impulse, the intent of the Revolution notwithstanding all that has happened since are widely extended and deeply rooted. Most of them have resisted the powerful hand of Bonaparte. They are more than a match for the feebler uncertain devices of their adversaries. . . . But I am convinced that those rights of mankind which in 1789 have been the blessing of the end of the last century shall before the end of the present one be the undisputed creed and insured property not only of this but of every European nation.

Louis XVIII arrived, and quickly made his intentions known. Freedom of the press was denied, and all feudal rights were restored to the aristocracy, which had lost these privileges during the Revolution. The Bourbons were making every effort to turn the clock back a quarter of a century.

Lafayette went to the Tuileries, and in the presence of the court informed the new king that such reactionary acts were stupid and harmful to the welfare of the country. Then he delivered an impassioned plea for liberty.

Had he been anyone but General Lafayette he might well have been imprisoned for his temerity. But the Bourbons were proceeding cautiously and did not want to arouse the ire of liberals everywhere by making Lafayette a martyr again. After he limped off to Diane de Simiane's house he was informed that he would not be welcome at the Tuileries again.

A short time later the daughter of Louis XVI subsidized the

writing and publication of a pamphlet attacking Lafayette. This document claimed that he alone had been responsible for the fall of the monarchy during the Revolution, that he had conspired with radicals while he was entrusted with the command of the National Guard.

The pamphlet was published on March 18, 1815 Two days later, before Lafayette could reply to it, Napoleon escaped from Elba, landed in the south of France, and marched to Paris with an ever increasing crowd at his heels. For the second time Louis XVIII decided the climate elsewhere would be healthier and departed in haste.

Lafayette stayed in Paris. He was uncertain whether Napoleon was a lesser evil than the Bourbons, but he saw an opportunity to establish a new, more liberal government under the returned emperor, and he was willing to work to that end. A reconstituted Chamber of Deputies was formed, and he accepted the post of vice-chairman, at least until he learned the Emperor's intentions.

Napoleon wanted the Chamber's support, and went there immediately after his return to make an address. For the first time in more than a decade he and Lafayette came face to face. "I haven't had the pleasure of seeing you for twelve years," Napoleon said.

Lafayette was equally cool. "Yes," he replied, "it has been a long time."

They never spoke again.

Napoleon made many glib promises, but Lafayette saw through them and, sickened by the public's gullibility, withdrew to La Grange. There, a few days later, he received a letter from Benjamin Constant, a writer who was working on a draft of a new constitution and who tried to convince him that Napoleon's conversion to the cause of liberty was genuine.

Lafayette's reply is significant because it summarizes his lifelong convictions:

It is only possible to be the active head of a free people in a republic if, as president or director, one is submitted to constant criticism and legal responsibility. It is only possible to be a constitutional monarch when inviolable, that is inactive, and nothing but the elector of the responsible ministers who are in consequence the judges of each order they receive from the king. A different situation is doubtless preferable not only for Napoleon but for every man who loves action and glory. . . .

Do you believe that either of these positions would long suit a character so impetuous, so enterprising and so impatient of contradiction? No liberty can exist in a country unless there be a representation freely and broadly elected, disposing of the raising and the spending of the public funds, making all laws, organizing all military forces, and with power to dissolve those forces, deliberating with open doors, in debates published in newspapers; unless there be complete liberty of the Press, supported by everything which guarantees personal, individual liberty; unless all offenses are removed from exceptional tribunals and submitted even independently of the will of the legislature to the justice of juries suitably formed. The civil crimes of soldiers, too, must be dealt with and the system of their penal discipline voted by the assemblies. . . .

If you have any influence on the work of those who make the constitution do not allow the elective principle for municipalities, justices of the peace, county and municipal councils to be tampered with: remember all your wise thoughts about the election of the Chamber of Deputies; do not leave to the prosecutor the formation of the list of juries. . . .

Let the counties and municipalities do all that can be entrusted to them. Do not forget the Mutiny Bill. Organize the National Guard. Re-read the law of the Constituent Assembly on the right of peace and war. Allow me to ask how you will form the Chamber of Peers? Even supposing you give preference, despite Hume's opinion, to the principle of hereditary legislators and even in some cases of hereditary judges, will you find in the more notable part of the nation a hereditary element which would be preferable to a Senate elected for life? Let me suggest another heresy against your opinions: it is that some pay, thirty francs for a day's service, for example, such as is the custom in the American Congress, is a system preferable to the English which makes all deputies pay their own expenses. I believe it will be easy to secure the liberty and equality of worship. The government will maintain the nomination of the principal ministers, but it would save itself much trouble and many quarrels if it left the choice and payment of inferior ministers to the municipalities or to assemblies of mere citizens. . . .

While Lafayette sat in his study at La Grange contemplating the establishment of an ideal government, Napoleon spent the first portion of what would become known as the Hundred Days reorganizing his administration and gathering a new army for the inevitable resumption of hostilities with the coalition.

On April 21, after an exchange of messages, Joseph Bonaparte, the brother of the Emperor, who had been on friendlier terms with Lafayette than any other member of the family, came to La Grange. There, in a talk that lasted for many hours, he frankly asked for Lafayette's support.

Lafayette was forced to admit that, in a choice between the Emperor and the Bourbons, Napoleon was the lesser evil.

Joseph tried to convince him that Napoleon's conversion to liberty was genuine. The Emperor, he said, had to leave Paris in order to meet his enemies in the field, and he wanted to leave the government in responsible hands. Therefore he was establishing a new legislature—a reconstituted Chamber of Deputies and a reconstituted Senate. He offered Lafayette a dukedom and the leadership of the upper body.

Lafayette refused, but did allow himself to be persuaded to become a candidate for the Chamber of Deputies. The following month he was elected without opposition, and returned to Paris with a mandate to prepare what Joseph had promised would be the most liberal constitution in all the world.

The new parliament convened officially on June 7. Napoleon presided, and in a short speech he charged deputies and senators with the task of preparing the constitution without delay. He and Lafayette did not speak, and that same day the Emperor joined his armies.

On June 17 and 18 a titanic battle was waged in cow pastures near Brussels, and Napoleon, although outnumbered and lacking ammunition, almost triumphed, but was defeated by the combined might of the British Duke of Wellington and the Prussian Marshal Blücher. Before the dust settled on Waterloo the Emperor was in his carriage, hurrying back to Paris to see what he could salvage of his regime.

The Parliament was in a turmoil, with members of both houses desperately trying to protect themselves. No one knew what would happen next, and such men as Fouché and Sieyès sought hedges against the future.

One man knew what needed to be done. Lafayette's calm was monumental as he demanded that both houses immediately pass legislation placing all of the reins of government in their own hands. The National Guard should be mustered for defense purposes alone, and foreign nations should be told that France wanted peace and only peace, but would fight again if invaded.

Another speaker rose to ask if Lafayette hadn't omitted something from his calculations—the Emperor.

"The Emperor," Lafayette said, "must abdicate without delay."

One of Napoleon's brothers, exhausted and probably frightened, tactlessly accused France of lacking endurance.

Lafayette jumped to his feet again, and this time he did not speak quietly. "Prince," he said, "that is a calumny. By what right do you dare to accuse the nation of levity, of want of perseverance in the Emperor's interest? The nation has followed him on the fields of Italy, over the burning sands of Egypt, in the immense plains of Germany, across the frozen deserts of Russia. Six hundred thousand Frenchmen lie on the shores of the Ebro and the Tagus. How many have fallen on the banks of the Danube, the Elbe, the Niemen, and the Moscova? The nation has followed him in fifty battles, in his defeats as in his victories, and for doing so we have to mourn the blood of three million Frenchmen."

Napoleon was furious when Lafayette's words were reported to him, but he had other matters on his mind and did not reply. He continued to temporize while he sought some new formula that would permit him to keep his throne.

Again Lafayette rose in the Chamber of Deputies and demanded the Emperor's abdication, saying it was inevitable and that every day's delay was harmful to the nation's interests. Speaker after speaker followed his example.

The two houses formed a joint committee to deal with the problem, and this group decided that a representative should confront the Emperor and inform him that Parliament demanded his resignation. Most members were still so much in awe of Napoleon that they were afraid of telling him to his face what they had voted, so they elected Lafayette, the one man who feared no one.

Napoleon refused to receive him.

The following day, when the confused and disturbed parliament met again, Lafayette offered a solution. At his instigation a brief letter was sent to the Emperor, under the signature of Gilbert Lafayette, informing him he would be dethroned if he did not abdicate.

Napoleon finally was forced to concede defeat, and on June 22 he stepped down for the second time.

The Parliament felt it was essential to form a temporary government for the purpose of negotiating with the victorious allies, and two names were placed in nomination for the post of provisional president, Lafayette and Fouché. Lafayette refused to campaign for himself, thinking it immodest. Fouché was a wily politician seeking to ensure his own future safety, so he was elected by a vote of 102 to 69. Lafayette was given the title of minister of war, and was instructed to attend the almost impossible task of negotiating the best possible terms with the military commanders of the victorious coalition.

Lafayette remained prominent in the thoughts of Napoleon during his years of bitter exile on the dreary island of St. Helena, and he pronounced his own valedictory summation of the man he had never been able to subdue: "He was a man without talents, civil or military; narrow mind, hypocritical character, dominated by vague ideas of liberty, undigested and ill thought out. Still, in private life Lafayette was an honest man. His good nature ever made him the dupe of men and things. His arousing of the Chamber after Waterloo lost us everything."

Others held a higher opinion of him. The Duke of Wellington and Tsar Alexander of Russia replied to his requests for a conference by saying they would be delighted to dine with him after they reached Paris. They were determined to occupy the city before talking about peace terms, but both made it plain that they were eager to make his acquaintance.

With nothing better to occupy him, Lafayette stayed in the Chamber, and at his instigation a "constitutional manifesto" was issued on July 5. In essence this strange document reaffirmed the principles of 1789. The leaders of the allied coalition thought the members were whistling in the dark. Thinking Frenchmen disagreed. Everyone realized that Louis XVIII would be returned to the throne in a few days, and that Lafayette was reminding the nation of its heritage before the forces of reaction took control again. Some of the Bourbon supporters believed they were being baited, but the Comte d'Artois recognized Lafayette's motive: The reactionaries were being notified that the spirit of liberty had not been extinguished.

On July 8, when the deputies arrived at the Chamber for their morning session, they found the doors locked, with armed British troops on duty in the courtyard. Lafayette immediately invited his colleagues to join him in a rump session at the house of Mme de Simiane, but most of them were too discouraged and tired to put up even this token show of resistance.

The victorious allies gave a number of dinner parties during their sojourn in Paris, and Lafayette was invited to most of these affairs, his name being omitted from the list only when the Comte d'Artois was to be present. On one occasion he found himself seated directly across the table from Napoleon's first wife, who was still being called the Empress Josephine.

"Wellington," he later said, "told me he approved of the imprisonment of the Spanish Parliament. I never liked him after that, but I suspect the dislike was mutual."

Tsar Alexander, the most enlightened of European kings,

was more his kind of man. "If only the Bourbons had listened to his advice," Lafayette said. "I told him that misfortune must have mended their ways. 'Mended their ways?' Alexander answered. 'They are uncorrected and incorrigible. Only the Duc d'Orléans has liberal views; as for the others, they are hopeless. It is not my fault that we have brought them back; they seemed to spring on us from every side. I tried to make the King give up his pretended nineteen years of reigning and other absurdities of the kind. But what could I do?' "

The visiting kings and generals departed, leaving France to the mercies of the Bourbons, and Lafayette promptly retreated to La Grange. There he stayed for three years, his official silence emphasizing his opposition to the counterrevolution. His policy was precisely what it had been during Napoleon's reign.

He entertained frequently, often with Diane de Simiane acting as his hostess, and it was not uncommon for twenty to thirty guests to sit down at his table. He was a gracious host, but the atmosphere was somewhat austere, as Lafayette frowned on exuberance and bad manners. His politics might be too advanced for the age, but in social intercourse he leaned in the direction of old-fashioned formality.

He permitted no gossip about the court under his roof, and guests who insisted on indulging in such small talk were not made welcome at La Grange again. He allowed no discussion of Bourbon policies or state affairs, either. Instead, he deliberately created an image of himself as a man who stood for principle.

Often he led the company in talk about such subjects as prison reform, which he ardently advocated. And the mere mention of slavery was enough to cause him to deliver a long and impassioned monologue in which he denounced the institution. Most of his guests, including British Whigs and liberals from every nation in Europe, felt as he did, and younger men began making pilgrimages to his castle.

Lafayette was ahead of his time in many of his views. He believed all citizens should be granted the franchise, whether or not they owned extensive property. He was one of the first in France to advocate giving women the vote, a view so radical that even his progressive friends were shocked. He was a firm believer in free trade among nations, and felt that a freely elected international parliament could be utilized as an instrument to prevent new wars.

He was convinced, too, that the wealthy had an obligation to help those who were less fortunate. When a severe economic depression threatened thousands with starvation in 1817, he distributed wheat and rye to seven hundred peasants, even though his generosity depleted his own granaries. Then he went to Chavaniac to do the same thing for the peasants there. The Bourbons suspected he had ulterior motives and was trying to buy popularity. When their attitude was reported to him he made one of his rare comments about them. "I do not expect the Tuileries to understand ordinary human compassion," he said. "Such sentiments are beneath them."

The Bourbons had not found it possible to turn back the clock as far as they wished. Literacy was rising, many thousands kept themselves informed about the state of the world and the nation by reading newspapers, including those published abroad when the French press was censored, and it had proved impossible to abolish the Chamber of Deputies.

Benjamin Constant, whose voice was one of the most liberal in Parisian journalism, became Lafayette's disciple during the hectic spring and summer of 1815, and thereafter was a frequent visitor to La Grange. He was convinced the time was ripe for the voice of freedom to be heard, and he disagreed with Lafayette's attitude that only through silence could tyranny be opposed. Constant, more than anyone else, was responsible for Lafayette's sudden and unexpected emergence from retirement.

15

A SMALL BAND of liberals sat in the Chamber of Deputies, trying in vain to make their voices heard. Badly outnumbered by the Ultras, as the followers of the Bourbons were called, they were timid, leaderless, and confused. The Comte d'Artois, the real ruler because of the chronic illness of Louis XVIII, was smugly satisfied: The Chamber was suiting his purposes, and other nations could not claim that opposition was being stifled.

Thanks to Benjamin Constant's prodding and the nagging of his own conscience, Lafayette agreed, in the late summer of 1818, to seek election to the Chamber. The alarmed Tuileries promptly made a substantial contribution to his opponent, and Lafayette himself seemed to make the task of the Ultras easier by refusing to campaign. The people knew him, he said, and would vote accordingly. They did, and he was elected by an overwhelming majority.

On December 1, 1818, Deputy Lafayette appeared at the Chamber in the blue uniform with silver collar worn by the members. Every seat in the visitors' galleries was taken, hundreds of others clamored for admission, and a crowd of thousands clustered outside to cheer the Hero of Two Worlds as he returned to the arena. He created a sensation when he took the oath of office, too, with deputies and peers alike throwing their hats into the air. His undiminished popularity was a cause of great concern to the Bourbons.

They had good reason to be worried. Lafayette now had a public forum for the expression of his views, and he was the Lafayette of old, a man of unyielding principle who fought for liberty and against repression. Only twenty-four hours after his return he served notice that the battle was joined. He announced that he was opposed to any attempt to restrict the election laws. He introduced a bill, probably drawn up by Constant, to extend and guarantee the freedom of the press. And he announced his opposition to extravagance in the national budget, indicating that the heavy spending by the royal family should be curbed and that funds be appropriated instead to strengthen and enlarge French industries.

A few months later, in 1819, Constant was elected as a deputy, and immediately became Lafayette's lieutenant. Together they battled for a free press, complete freedom of religion, and the extension of the franchise, at that time limited to about 100,000 voters out of a total population of almost 30,000,000.

The liberals in Parliament may have been a small group, but they spoke for what would prove, eleven years later, to be a majority of the French people. Overnight Lafayette became the most popular man in the country again; the early days of the Revolution were being repeated, and he was regarded as the savior of the poor, the champion of the middle class. His long retirement had not dimmed his stature, and radical pamphlets, which he disavowed, urged Paris to overthrow Louis

XVIII and make Lafayette president of a new republic.

Not since the days of Marie Antoinette had Lafayette been so roundly condemned in the Tuileries, but the Comte d'Artois, the future Charles X, disagreed with his relatives. "I have known Lafayette since we were schoolmates," he said, "and we share the virtue of consistency. You admire me because my values are what they were, but you condemn him as a turncoat. That is unfair. His standards are unchanged, too, and I hope he bakes over the fires of hell for all eternity."

The King's nephew, the Duc de Berry, was assassinated by a fanatic, and while the secret police took advantage of their opportunity to arrest and imprison scores of suspected dissidents, the Ultras renewed their efforts to limit the franchise. Lafayette lost his air of objective tranquillity, and delivered an emotionally charged address in the Chamber, saying in part:

"We are tired of revolutions, satiated with glories, but we shall not allow ourselves to be deprived of our dearly bought rights and interests. Our youth demands liberty with a reasoned and therefore all the more irresistible ardor. Do not force them by threatening to deprive them of all the useful results of the Revolution to seize for themselves the sacred sheaf of the principles of eternal truth and sovereign justice."

He was doing more than indulging in parliamentary rhetoric when he referred to the younger generation. A new movement was sweeping across Europe, in part created and emphatically exacerbated by the repressions emanating from the creature of the allied powers, the Congress of Vienna. In 1819 or thereabouts a new technique for fighting the reactionaries was developed in Naples, where it became fashionable for young men to join secret societies dedicated to the cause of liberty. Similar organizations came into being in France, and by 1820 the country was honeycombed with them. Many were informal clubs, their membership principally made up of university students, and almost without exception they took the name of Lafayette in vain, proposing that he be made president of a republican France. No correspondence or documents of any other kind exist to indicate that he even knew his name was being used.

The secret police learned of the existence of these organizations in 1820, and swiftly disbanded them, throwing some of the students into prison. The Bourbons, including Artois, were convinced that Lafayette was directly involved, but were afraid to make any moves against him. Their hold on the throne was precarious, they knew they had little popular support, and the arrest of Lafayette could have sparked another revolution. No member of the royal family had forgotten the guillotine.

If he was truly guilty of treason, that fact had to be proved beyond any doubt. An attempt was made early in 1821, when letters he and Constant had written were produced at the trial of a political dissident. Lafayette was called to testify, and readily admitted authorship of the letters in his handwriting. The regime believed he had been cornered, but he pointed out that he had said nothing in his correspondence that he had not already declared in public from the floor of the Chamber of Deputies. Any potential charges against him were forgotten.

He may or may not have been involved in a far more serious conspiracy that developed later in 1821. A group of dedicated republicans planned to overthrow the Bourbons by establishing a provisional government with Lafayette at its head. They intended to establish two temporary working headquarters, one at Saumur in the west and the other at Belfort in the east.

At the very least Lafayette knew of this plot, and was sufficiently interested to investigate it in depth. Apparently he was invited to Belfort for the purpose. As his stiff leg was bothering him, he made the journey by carriage. When he was only a short distance from the town he was told that the secret police had learned of the scheme, and even now were in Belfort, where everyone implicated was being arrested.

Lafayette was forced to flee on horseback, leaving his carriage behind. The vehicle bore his crest, and had the police found it they would have had the evidence against him they were seeking. His friends and admirers in the area hid the coach in a barn and did not return it to him at La Grange until some months had passed.

Eight of the known conspirators were sent to the guillotine, in spite of Lafayette's strenuous efforts to save them, and Benjamin Constant spent a brief period in prison. Lafayette had never been the sort of man to engage in conspiracy and it is difficult to believe he played an active role in the plot; besides, by this time it must have occurred to him that the mere use of his name gave the police an excuse to act. If he did at this late date permit himself to become directly involved in the conspiracy, he learned that he was too old to be a party to clandestine operations.

In September 1821 Lafayette delivered one of his most pungent speeches in the Chamber. The budget allocations to members of the royal family and their households, he said, were reminiscent of the profligacy at Versailles in the time of Louis XV. He deplored the sums granted to the secret police, and attacked that organization as "a great and perpetual administrative lie, whether royal or imperial I do not care. There is no doubt that that insolent and vile organization has done more than all other causes put together to poison public morals, encourage domestic betrayals and private crimes, to excite conspiracies and disorders. . . ." He concluded by demanding free public education for all children and increased pay for the army and navy, and requested that monastic orders in the pay of foreign powers be required to close down.

The climax of Lafayette's career as a deputy came in late November 1821. A fellow liberal, Jacques Antoine Manuel, made a speech the Ultras regarded as seditious, and the following day he was denied his seat in the Chamber. Manuel ignored the injunction, and after he took his accustomed place a squad of the National Guard under the command of a captain was sent in to arrest and remove him.

Lafayette, revered as the founder of the National Guard, lost his temper. Under no circumstances, he thundered, did troops of any kind have the right to invade the Chamber of Deputies, and it was a crime against the nation for the National Guard, dedicated to the preservation of the peace on behalf of all Frenchmen, to participate in such activity.

Pointing a long forefinger at the troops, he said, "I order you to leave!"

Members of the squad marched out, and only the officer stayed behind, but after a moment's indecision he too bolted.

The prestige of the regime was involved, and soon a group of secret policemen in civilian clothes appeared. Surrounding Manuel, they forced him to leave.

Lafayette jumped to his feet. "The present rulers of France," he said, "make a mockery of the very name of liberty!"

Turning on his heel, he stalked out of the Chamber, followed by more than sixty of his colleagues. "The scene," he later said, "was worthy of the early days of the Revolution."

Instead of going to Diane de Simiane's house, he emphasized his withdrawal by riding straight to La Grange, and he never returned to the Chamber of Deputies. His three-year career as a parliamentarian was at an end.

The Ultras and their masters rejoiced, and some liberals thought Lafayette was sulking, while others believed he was using his old tactics. He was doing neither. He wrote Jefferson:

> If I continue on my present course, the friends of liberty here will force me to lead them into a new revolution, and I cannot allow my hands to be stained with this tired nation's blood. Only by staying close to my own hearth can this fresh catastrophe be averted. The insolent stupidity of the Bourbons is so great they will destroy themselves.

Lafayette's new retirement was unique. Twice before he had taken refuge in a silence that France and the outside world alike had recognized as disapproval. This time neither his fellow countrymen nor outsiders permitted him to separate himself from politics and live in peace. At the age of sixty-four he had become Europe's greatest living symbol of liberty, and the members of younger generations not only wanted to pay homage to him but actively sought his advice, help, and direct support.

He was wary in his dealings with the French patriots who came to La Grange, urging them not to lose faith while staying out of trouble. He was more direct in his relations with foreigners, contributing cash as well as advice to republicans from Naples and Milan who wanted to unify the Italian states under a new liberal constitution. He gave money, too, to Belgian and Hungarian nationalists, and carried on a vigorous correspondence with freedom lovers in Spain, Portugal, several of the German states, and Poland.

If he dealt in secret with many of these people, it was for their protection, not his own. Private messengers delivered and took away much of his mail so it would not fall into the hands of the police, and some of his visitors arrived at night, when they would not be recognized. With the forces of reaction still in control throughout Europe, liberty was a crime in many lands.

For himself, of course, Lafayette was as indifferent to danger as he had ever been. The Bourbons could not arrest him unless they could directly implicate him in a plot against the crown, and he was participating in no such projects. Even if he had been active in them, his prestige was so great that the Comte d'Artois would not have dared to punish him.

Liberals began to call Lafayette the "savior of liberty," and he relished the title. In fact, he enjoyed playing the role so much that he foolishly gave money to many young adventurers who simply took advantage of him. "He reached for his purse," Virginie said, "the very moment someone mentioned freedom to him."

This largesse, combined with his chronic inability to handle large sums of money, began to cause problems for him. His basic fortune was intact, but he had many mouths to feed and a large establishment to maintain, so he needed a substantial cash income. Only Adrienne could have put his affairs in order and curbed his generosity; his children tried to control him, but he paid no attention to them.

Finally they turned to Diane de Simiane for help, but she had listened to Lafayette admiringly for the better part of a half century without advising him or hauling him into line, and it was too late now to change the nature of their relationship. In fact, Mme de Simiane, who was herself in her sixties, was growing tired, and came to La Grange less frequently. Too loyal to Lafayette to curtsy before the Bourbons at the Tuileries, she was spending most of her time at her own country estate. The fires were banked, and she was moving serenely into old age.

Lafayette, however, still regarded himself as a man in his

prime, and a loss of weight helped him to look like one. Only his cane betrayed him when he walked. He had a quick eye for pretty girls, and enjoyed flirting with friends of his elder grand-daughters who came to visit, much to the amusement of the entire family.

His sheep and cattle were regarded as among the best in Europe, and his crops were more plentiful than those of other farmers in his neighborhood. He remained interested in farm-ing, but George had taken active charge of the estate, and he confined himself to spending an hour or two riding around the property in a small gig each day, with some of his younger grandchildren in tow.

Occasionally he showed signs of eccentricity. Adrienne had loved flowers, and during her lifetime there had been extensive beds of flowers surrounding the château at La Grange. After her death Lafayette had allowed them to go untended, and in 1817 had decided the land was being wasted, so he ordered vegetables planted there.

One day in the spring of 1822 he discovered that a new gardener had put in several long rows of rosebushes, and he flew into a rage. "Tear out those ugly bushes," he shouted, "and put in flat beans and maize. I want this place to look attractive!"

The bewildered gardener went to Emilie, who shared her late mother-in-law's love of flowers and recently, on a trip to Chavaniac, had supervised the planting of several hundred tulip bulbs that Dutch patriots had sent to Lafayette as a gift. "No one," she said, "ever crosses the General. Do as he di-rects."

The only person who had the courage to contradict La-fayette was his one grandson to date, Gilbert de Lasteyrie. Lafayette paid no attention to Virginie's complaints that he spoiled the child. He delighted in teaching the boy riding and

fencing, but one day, when they were practising swordsman-
ship, the little boy went too far.

"Grandpapa," he said, "your riposte is clumsy."

Lafayette's renown as a swordsman was so great that no man
had ever been courageous enough to challenge him to a duel.
Now he lowered his blade, his eyes suddenly cold as he looked
at his grandson. "So, Gilbert? We shall see," he said.

They crossed blades again, and suddenly little Gilbert's
sword flew out of his hand. At almost the same instant his
grandfather's tipped foil touched his heart.

"You, sir, are dead," Lafayette declared.

Gilbert ran from the room weeping. Thereafter, much to the
relief of his parents, his arrogance vanished and his demands
on his grandfather were muted.

Playing with his grandchildren gave Lafayette his only pleas-
ures in 1822 and 1823. The Bourbons, thanks to their ever
growing secret police, were firmly in control of France, and a
sense of political apathy gripped the country. Freedoms were
limited, but no one seemed to care. The cause of liberty was
flourishing nowhere else, either, in spite of the money and time
Lafayette was devoting to the cause.

His own financial affairs were becoming more precarious,
and he was unwilling to listen to George, who had inherited
his mother's talents and might have been able to establish
greater order. The family was horrified, one night at dinner,
when Lafayette calmly expressed his intention of selling some
lands in Brittany so he could pay his debts. Until that evening
no one had realized how serious his situation had become.

Early in January 1823 Diane de Simiane slipped in her
bathtub and broke her arm. The roads were icy and treacher-
ous, but Lafayette went to her the moment he received the
news, and spent the next month at her side.

When he returned home in February he was tired, and for the first time his buoyant spirit was subdued. He was growing old, he confided to his daughters and daughter-in-law, and he no longer was able to hope that the spirit of liberty would flourish.

Thereafter he went into a mental depression, sometimes refusing to answer his mail and spending long hours sitting in a chair, staring out at the fields of La Grange. Emilie noted that he spent more and more time meditating in Adrienne's bedroom.

Suddenly, in the late spring of 1824, a miracle occurred. Lafayette received a letter from an old friend, President James Monroe of the United States. On his own behalf, Monroe wrote, as well as that of the Congress and the American people, Lafayette was cordially invited to pay a visit to the land whose freedom he had done so much to attain. The fiftieth anniversary of independence would be empty without him, and the United States government was pleased to put a warship at his disposal for the voyage across the Atlantic.

All at once the sun came out again, and one of the most extraordinary chapters in Lafayette's long life was about to begin.

16

THE LONG VISIT paid by Lafayette to the United States, beginning in 1824 and ending in 1826, was a personal triumph that ultimately exerted incalculable influence in France and other European nations. It is no exaggeration to say that the repercussions were among the direct causes of the revolutions that broke out in France and elsewhere in 1830.

Democracy and its handmaiden, personal liberty, had been stifled on the Continent since the fall of Napoleon, and even in Great Britain the forces of reaction were in control. Only in America was the experiment in freedom flourishing. By 1824 there were more than 11,000,000 people in the United States, and the population was expanding at a rate of about 350,000 per year. The very name of the country had become synonymous with freedom, and Europe's downtrodden were attracted to her shores in ever increasing numbers. Partly as a result of the publicity that attended Lafayette's reception, the rate of immigration almost doubled in the decade that followed his extraordinary tour.

He was a legend in America even before he arrived, his unselfish contributions to the nation's independence duly recorded in textbooks and taught in schools. The last living major general who had fought in the Revolution, he had become a symbol of all that the country represented. The aged Jefferson called him "the doyen of the soldiers of liberty of the world."

The Eighteenth Congress offered to make a navy frigate available to Lafayette for his Atlantic crossing, but he declined the honor, saying that acceptance would be an extravagance and a burden on the American taxpayer. His thoughtful note showed an understanding of the temperament of the American people, and struck precisely the right tone for his visit. He graciously accepted a large suite on an American commercial vessel, the *Cadmus,* which was commanded by the son of one of his former officers.

He left La Grange on July 10, 1824, accompanied by his son and a secretary. The purpose of his journey had become known, and troops were stationed along the road to Le Havre to prevent possible public demonstrations. Thousands gathered at the dock, and silently removed their hats as he sailed.

A sloop-of-war stationed off the American coast for the purpose caught sight of the *Cadmus* on the morning of August 14, and by the time Lafayette came ashore late that afternoon virtually the entire population of New York, now a city of more than 250,000, turned out to give him a riotous welcome. He wore the uniform of a major general of the Continental line. Tears came into his eyes as bands played and he reviewed a military honor guard, and the crowds went wild.

The Union was now composed of twenty-four states and he went to all of them, traveling thousands of miles by carriage, horseback, steamboat, river barge, and even mule train. The first part of his visit took place during the last months of the administration of President James Monroe, a period known as the Era of Good Feeling, when there were no political disputes of consequence in the nation, so Lafayette saw a harmonious democracy at work. He was entertained by two former presidents, Jefferson and Madison, by President John Quincy Adams both before and after he took office, and by two future presidents, Andrew Jackson and Martin Van Buren. General Jackson, at their Nashville meeting, wept as he presented the guest with a precious memento of his own, a pair of dueling pistols that had belonged to George Washington, and called the experience "the greatest moment of my life."

Between mid-August and the end of the year he visited New Haven, Providence, Boston, Concord, Albany, Philadelphia, Washington, and Richmond. Everywhere, day after day, he heard cannon booming in the thirteen-gun salute due a major general; everywhere bands played, dinners and balls and assemblies and barbecues and picnics and fandangos were held in his honor. Everywhere he heard glowing speeches of welcome and responded to them; everywhere he received gifts ranging from trinkets to swords to livestock.

In September, on his sixty-seventh birthday, he was the guest of the Society of the Cincinnati, the order of Revolutionary War officers, who saluted him with a fireworks display that illuminated a replica of his château at La Grange. Other receptions were equally elaborate. In Trenton, for example, he was welcomed by twenty-four young ladies in costume whose headdresses were the official seals of each of the states.

Fears were expressed for Lafayette's physical well-being early in the tour, and certainly George and the secretary frequently were exhausted. But the Marquis, as he was universally called by his hosts, enjoyed himself so much that he never tired, and he seemed to grow younger day by day. He was busy at least sixteen hours each day, sometimes much longer, but he needed only a few hours of sleep and almost never rested during the day.

His appetite was prodigious. At a typical breakfast he ate a bowl of porridge, a half-dozen fried perch, and a roast duck, which he washed down with ale. Banquets of as many as a dozen courses were common. Sides of beef and venison were prepared over pits, and his plate was piled high with local delicacies. He ate everything, and held his own when innumerable toasts were consumed. He listened intently to the speeches in which identical sentiments were expressed, and there was never a hint of weariness in his vigorous responses. He danced with hundreds of ladies, flattered thousands with his gallantry, and lost no opportunity to kiss a pretty girl. When he visited the sites of battles in which he had fought, his path was strewn with flowers.

In Washington he was an official guest at the President's mansion, known as the White House since it had been rebuilt after being destroyed by the British in the War of 1812. He inspected literally every government building, and in December he created a precedent when he addressed the Senate and House of Representatives meeting in a joint session, the first foreigner ever to do so. In the next century and a quarter more than forty other distinguished guests would follow him to that rostrum.

A special high point of his journey was a visit to Mount Vernon. At his specific request no one accompanied him to Washington's grave—his son paid his own respects there later —and he stayed there for an hour, alone with his private thoughts.

Joseph Bonaparte, Napoleon's brother, was living in exile near Trenton. Lafayette's relations with him had always been cordial, and he called on him there. They spoke together for several hours behind closed doors. Neither man ever revealed what was said.

Almost everywhere Lafayette insisted on speaking English, but at Monticello, out of deference to his aged host, who wanted to converse in French, he reverted to his native tongue. A similar experiment was less successful at nearby Montpelier, the estate of James Madison. Like so many others, Americans and foreigners alike, he was enchanted by the former first lady, but Dolly Madison's French made him wince, and he gently guided their conversations back to the safer ground of English.

Although Lafayette was intent on continuing his travels through the winter, he was persuaded to spend January and a portion of February in Washington. The roads were impassable seas of mud, so he contented himself with dining daily with senators and congressmen, retiring President Monroe, and President-elect Adams. His pride prevented him from revealing to anyone that his financial situation at home was precarious, but at one time or another his son and his secretary let the secret slip. Members of the government were horrified, unable to tolerate the thought that Lafayette might be in want, so prompt remedial action was taken.

By unanimous vote the Congress made him a gift of $250,000, the equivalent of more than five times that amount a century and a quarter later, and he was also given a 25,000-acre tract of federal lands. The gift was so generous that he was embarrassed, but Monroe and Adams were able to persuade him not to reject it, arguing that their compatriots would be insulted. He swallowed his pride, capitulated, and never again knew financial need.

In February 1825 he resumed his travels. He was thrilled by his visit to Fayetteville, North Carolina, the first town named for him. Later he attended dedication ceremonies in Lafayette, Indiana, and Lafayette, Louisiana, and was overjoyed when a new university in Pennsylvania was given his name. Few men anywhere had been accorded such honors in their own life- times.

His hosts were most impressed by the fact that Lafayette did not behave like a foreign aristocrat. He so completely under- stood the principles of American democracy that he was indeed an American; equally important, he had commanded Ameri- can troops in combat, and he knew the people as well as he knew the French. When he went to a picnic attended by men in shirtsleeves, he removed his own coat and rolled up his sleeves. When a creek had to be forded he waded through mud with the rest, then insisted on cleaning his own boots. No detail of daily life escaped his notice, and when he particularly en- joyed a dish, he asked for the recipe so he could take it with him to France.

Again and again he heard his hosts beg him to settle in the United States and stay for the rest of his days. He was assured of seats in both the Senate and House of Representatives, and John Quincy Adams even indicated that a place awaited him in the Cabinet. He was deeply touched, and occasionally he wavered, but the temptations ultimately strengthened his basic resolve. Freedom and the rights of man were secure in Amer- ica, he told his friends, but the struggle was still being waged against the Bourbons at home, and he would be remiss in his duty if he failed to return to France and continue the fight for liberty there.

He merely shrugged when it was suggested to him that he had stood on the ramparts for almost half a century and that he deserved to rest on his laurels. "No soldier in the armies of liberty," he told Andrew Jackson, "can afford to lay aside his sword until the last battle is won." His sincere words were printed in scores of American newspapers, and won him still greater popularity. Copies found their way to Europe, where heartened liberals formed new organizations dedicated to the cause of freedom. On both sides of the Atlantic thousands of newborn baby boys were named Gilbert Lafayette.

The French government pondered the question of whether to readmit him to the country when he returned home. Most members of the Bourbon family and their supporters were in favor of forcing him to go into exile for the rest of his life, but the Comte d'Artois disagreed. "If the people are allowed to choose between Lafayette and me," he said, "it will be I who is sent into exile, and I'll be lucky if I escape with my life. I have no wish to emulate my late brother and Marie Antoinette, so I shall not make a martyr of Monsieur de Lafayette. Neither do I want the United States to declare war against us and seize our colonies in the West Indies, which would surely happen if we were to declare war against Lafayette. He is an unofficial member of the Chamber of Deputies, and the constituency he represents is America."

During Lafayette's absence from France, Louis XVIII died, and his brother ascended the throne as Charles X. Narrow-minded and bigoted, unable to realize that times had changed, this active champion of reaction was at least right in his assessment of his lifelong rival. The people of America were united in their unqualified support of Lafayette. American Indians traveled long distances on horseback and on foot to salute the man who had been the friend of their grandfathers. Slaves startled their masters by cheering the man who, they were told, had spent a lifetime demanding their freedom.

Lafayette traveled by steamer up the Mississippi River from New Orleans, then had an unexpected adventure on the Ohio

River when the vessel struck an underwater obstacle and sank. No one was injured, and he enjoyed the experience.

He arrived back in Boston on June 15, 1825, and two days later he was the principal speaker at the ceremonies marking the fiftieth anniversary of the Battle of Bunker Hill. A quarter of a million people were present for the occasion, and he marched at the head of the column of Revolutionary War veterans; a special contingent was made up of his own former troops, and tears came to his eyes when he saw these elderly men.

That night, at a banquet attended by more than four thousand, his natural ebullience reasserted itself. "Tonight," he said, "we celebrate the fiftieth anniversary of American independence. In another fifty years we shall drink to the emancipation of Europe."

Without exception the major newspapers of the United States published his words, and foreign legations duly reported them to their own superiors. Lafayette's views did not endear him to the crowned heads of Europe, and Charles X remarked, "Lafayette has never changed and will never change. He is as stubborn in his defense of the wrong as I am stubborn in my defense of the right."

The last portion of Lafayette's sojourn in the United States was less hectic than the earlier months had been. He spent most of his stay on the eastern seaboard, the part of the country he knew best, and he removed himself from the limelight as he visited friends in New England, New York, New Jersey, and Pennsylvania. In the main he avoided the big cities and spent his time at country houses, where he took his ease. Leaders of Catholic, Jewish, and Protestant groups, knowing how hard he had worked to establish true freedom of religion in France, invited him into their houses of worship, and he usually accepted. Frequently he was asked to deliver a sermon, and gave a short address in which he urged the members of the congregation to remain vigilant in the protection of their right to worship as they pleased.

By easy stages Lafayette made his way back to Virginia for a farewell visit to Thomas Jefferson, with whom he celebrated his sixty-eighth birthday, and he made a final pilgrimage to Mount Vernon. Again he visited Washington as the guest of President Adams, attending a long round of farewell parties in his honor that left him buoyant but exhausted the members of his own entourage and other young men.

Lafayette had accumulated so many gifts during his stay in America that the goods and livestock weighed several tons and could not be shipped on a commercial vessel. So he gratefully accepted the offer of a warship made by the President and the Congress. When he was piped aboard at Baltimore with full honors he wore his American uniform for the last time.

Lafayette arrived at Le Havre on a bitterly cold day in the winter of 1825–1826, and on his homeward journey he discovered that news of his reception in the United States had reached France. Large crowds gathered in Rouen and other cities to greet him and cheer him, ignoring the attempts of white-uniformed troops to silence them.

Paris was even more enthusiastic; tens of thousands of people lined the streets and applauded as his carriage passed. Royal troops could have choked off the demonstrations only at the risk of inciting large-scale riots. Lafayette's trip to America was already bearing unexpected fruit at home.

17

CHARLES X and his ministers were relieved when Lafayette limited his stay in Paris to a single night before hurrying home to his waiting family at La Grange. The Hero of Two Worlds represented a grave threat to the stability and security of the regime, and had he been anyone else he would have been either jailed or deported. But his arrest would have been the spark that might have caused an oppressed people to begin a new revolution, and the crown was afraid to touch him. The secret police could read his incendiary letters and make lists of the liberals who made pilgrimages to his estate, but he was beyond the grasp of the King, a symbol of liberty who had become a law unto himself.

Lafayette returned from the United States with a mission. He was no longer content to wait quietly for the swing of the pendulum, but was convinced that freedom would thrive only where it was encouraged by dedicated, fearless men. Well into his sixty-ninth year, he assumed the unofficial leadership of that cause, and began an extensive correspondence with liberals in the Italian and German states, the Austrian Empire, even in France itself. Sometimes, at home, he dined in private with earnest young men, excluding members of his family from the table for their own protection. If they did not know the identities of his guests, the secret police would be less likely to harass them.

By the time Lafayette returned home he had formed the conclusion that the best hopes for liberty lay in the New World, where his beloved United States had set the example. In the early days of Napoleon's empire he had met and influenced the brilliant Simón Bolívar, then a refugee from Spanish tyranny. Now Bolívar, the "George Washington of South America," had liberated a vast section of that continent, extending from the Caribbean to the border of Argentina, and a delighted Lafayette initiated a spirited correspondence with the man he called his "dear and respectable friend." Bolívar was very pleased to hear from him, and thereafter both men wrote regularly.

A financial depression that began in England in 1826 soon spread to the Continent, and its effects were severe. The middle class suffered heavy losses, the alarming rise in the price of bread caused the poor to go hungry, and neither the white-uniformed troops nor the secret police could prevent a growing hatred for Charles X. It was said the King had a dream in which Lafayette rode into Paris on a white horse.

Too late the ministers of the crown offered political concessions, but even these reforms lacked real substance. Lafayette could have aroused the people, but he still preferred orderly change to violence, and he refused to abandon the principles that had guided him for so many years.

By the summer of 1827 the political restlessness became worse, the country was still mired in the depression, and

Charles X at last agreed to call a new general election. Lafayette was persuaded to permit his name to be placed in nomination, and in early August 1827, a month before his seventieth birthday, he won a seat in the Chamber of Deputies.

Charles X might have saved his crown had he given in to public clamor and made Lafayette his prime minister, but he could not force himself to appoint a man whose views were so opposed to his own. Instead he gave the post to the Duc de Polignac, an archconservative who shared the King's myopic view of France and the world.

Lafayette was content to sit in the Chamber, where he frequently spoke cogently for the cause of liberty. He took no part in the day-to-day squabbles of younger men, and he urged fiery young opposition leaders not to push the country into a new civil war. "We are making progress," he said repeatedly. "For each two steps backward that France takes, we move three steps forward. The era of true liberty soon will be at hand."

Most of Lafayette's old friends were dead, so he needed new quarters of his own in Paris when the Chamber was in session. Members of the family bought a small house for him on the Rue d'Anjou and staffed it with servants from La Grange. Without his knowledge the younger members of the family privately worked out a schedule, and one or another "happened" to stay at the house whenever he was in the city. He was still in full command of his faculties, but the family felt safer when someone was on hand to keep an eye on him.

In the spring of 1828 Lafayette paid his last known visit to the estate of Diane de Simiane. Two of his grandchildren escorted him, and remained there with him for the ten days he spent with Mme de Simiane. If she and Lafayette saw each other at any time thereafter, their meeting is unrecorded.

The new Parliament, which had little power, met infrequently, and Lafayette spent the better part of his time at La Grange, conducting his extensive correspondence with liberals in many lands. His family life was active, too: He had thirteen grandchildren, most of whom lived either on the estate or nearby, and was beginning to acquire great-grandchildren at such a rapid rate that he was finding it difficult to remember their names.

In the autumn of 1829 the seventy-two-year-old Lafayette paid a visit to Chavaniac, and the temper of the times was reflected in the welcome given him in city after city, town after town. People lined the streets to cheer him, banquets and receptions were given in his honor, and he remarked mildly that he sometimes felt he was in America.

A word from him might have dethroned Charles X, and Lafayette knew it, so he was careful not to utter that word. As a deputy he had sworn to uphold the crown, and an oath was as sacred to him in 1829 as it had been in 1789. He delivered his most incendiary speech in Lyons, where he spoke with the bluntness that had characterized his long life: "No more concessions is what the official papers are saying. No more concessions the people of France will say in turn, and with a better right when it demands those institutions so long awaited which alone can guarantee the enjoyment of our imprescriptible rights. The force of every government exists only in the arms and in the purse of the citizens who comprise the nation. The French nation knows its rights and will know how to defend them."

Charles X had the Bourbon genius for misunderstanding his people, and Lafayette, sitting serenely at La Grange, wrote early in 1830 that a confrontation could not long be postponed between the crown and the Parliament. A frequent visitor to

La Grange that winter agreed with him. Louis Philippe, Duc d'Orléans and the King's cousin, was the one "sensible" member of the royal family. He dressed like a middle-class merchant, put on no airs, and made it a practice to walk unaccompanied rather than ride through the streets of Paris. He appeared dedicated to the cause of liberty, and paid lip service to it with enough fervor to win the admiration of Lafayette and other liberals.

Lafayette badly misjudged him, as did the people of France in the months ahead. What the Hero of Two Worlds, now in his seventy-third year, failed to take into account was that Louis Philippe was still a Bourbon. His family traits were less visible that those of his cousins, but were just as pronounced.

The confrontation Lafayette had predicted took place late in March, when 221 members of the Chamber, a majority, opposed the crown. King Charles dismissed Parliament and called for new elections. All 221 were reelected, but he still refused to grant the reforms they demanded.

Suddenly, at the beginning of the last week in July 1830, the citizens of Paris took matters into their own hands and a full-scale insurrection broke out. Lafayette rode into the city, escorted by two of his tall grandsons, and they had to climb over street barricades in order to reach the house on the Rue d'Anjou. The King, after the manner of Bourbons, called out the troops and waited for them to disperse the mobs.

The street fighting became worse, and by midweek a full-scale revolution was in progress. King Charles played whist with the Duc d'Anjou while in the Chamber speaker after speaker urged that a republic be established, with Lafayette as president. The old gentleman was approached, and promptly rebuked his colleagues by reminding them that in a republic officials were elected to office rather than appointed.

In spite of his determination to abide by the principles of legality that he had followed throughout his career, the entire country turned to him in its hour of crisis. In scenes reminiscent of the early days of the French Revolution he received a steady stream of callers. Messengers brought him word that the revolution was spreading to the provinces and men of every political persuasion, including royalists long opposed to him, begged him to assume authority as the only way to avoid chaos.

Lafayette held firm. The National Guard was being reconstituted, and when a number of his colleagues asked him to take command of the army of citizen-soldiers, he told them he would consent only if the Chamber voted him into office.

This was done, and a huge crowd gathered to watch and cheer as he rode to the Hôtel de Ville, suitably mounted on a white horse. His grandsons, whom he appointed as his aides, accompanied him when he went to take the oath of office from a municipal commission, in effect a provisional government. Meanwhile mobs were completing their self-appointed task of driving the disheartened royalist troops out of the city, and a frightened Charles X finally capitulated, indicating his willingness to grant freedom of speech, press, assemblage, and worship.

News of the King's surrender was brought to Lafayette at the Hôtel de Ville, where liberals were trying to persuade him to proclaim the establishment of a republic and monarchist moderates were urging him to use the opportunity to create a constitutional monarchy. He had the power to determine the future of France, and the fate of King Charles was in his hands. Realizing that the monarch was discredited, he declared, "All recognition is impossible. The royal family has ceased to reign."

Lafayette went to bed on the night of July 29 with the future still unresolved. The Chamber met on the morning of the thirtieth, but he absented himself from the session, feeling it would be inappropriate for him to appear in uniform. The situation became even more confused, with liberals urging the immediate establishment of a republic and moderate monarchists rallying around Louis Philippe, who had the courage to come to Paris from his house in the suburbs to see what he could do to further his own cause.

The house on the Rue d'Anjou was crowded with visitors. Republicans urged that the American Constitution be adapted for France; Louis Philippe's followers argued that only under a constitutional monarchy would France be able to prevent a new war with the reactionary regimes in control elsewhere in Europe.

Had he wished, Lafayette could have chosen a republic, certain that the people of Paris would have followed his advice, and there was no doubt that he would be elected president. On the other hand, the issue of war and peace was vital, and he felt it was urgent to prevent the formation of a new allied coalition against France. While he debated the issue with himself, Charles X quietly fled into new exile.

Charles de Rémusat, who was married to Virginie's eldest daughter, Pauline, finally came to Lafayette with the question no one else dared to put into words. "It is either you or the Duc d'Orléans," he said. "Which shall it be?"

Lafayette realized that at the age of seventy-three he lacked the strength and energy to create a new type of government and supervise its formation. "All I want is to be left in peace," he said. "If Orléans will agree to be a constitutional king, I am for him."

On the morning of July 31 General Lafayette rode to the Hôtel de Ville, cheered by hundreds of thousands of Parisians who felt certain the intended to proclaim the establishment of a republic. Members of the Chamber of Deputies milled around in the great hall, along with politicians of every party, military men, and industrialists. The crowd parted as Lafayette slowly made his way to an armchair, and he alone sat, king-maker or uncrowned king, founder and possible president of a French republic.

Louis Philippe came into the hall, and Lafayette rose from his chair to shake his hand. Everyone present noted that the old general did not bow, as one did to a monarch. Many men eavesdropped on their conversation.

"You know," Lafayette said, "that I am a republican, and that I regard the Constitution of the United States as the best ever devised."

"Of course," the Duc d'Orléans replied. "No one could live in the United States for years and not believe that. But do you think that, considering our present situation in France, we could adopt it as it now stands?"

"No," Lafayette said. "What we need in this country today is a popular throne surrounded by republican institutions— totally republican."

Louis Philippe nodded and murmured assent.

Lafayette believed Orléans had committed himself to the establishment of a constitutional monarchy, and so did most of the others in the great hall. Later, after demonstrating that he was as much of a Bourbon as his deposed cousin, Louis Philippe insisted he had not agreed to anything.

The acceptance of the new regime by the people was a necessary blessing, and Lafayette, who had not lost his flair for the dramatic, led Louis Philippe onto a balcony. There he thrust a tricolor flag into the hands of Orléans, in effect crowning him, and the crowd screamed its approval.

The issue was settled, and Louis Philippe mounted the throne with a new title: He was king of the French rather than King of France.

Lafayette was satisfied. He had averted a full-scale revolution, and a return to the days of the Terror had been avoided. What was equally important was that a constitutional monarchy had been created at last, or so he believed. Only two days earlier, when taking the oath of office as commander of the National Guard, he had said, "I shall make no profession of faith. My sentiments are known."

His greatest weakness throughout his entire life had been his willingness to believe that other men were as honest and forthright as he proved himself to be. It literally did not cross his mind that Louis Philippe had no intention of establishing the kind of government that Lafayette envisioned. In his delight at the way the crisis ended, the old gentleman wrote to a friend in London, "We have made a beautiful and quick revolution. . . . All its glory belongs to the people of Paris."

In the weeks following the accession of Louis Philippe, Lafayette remained the center of attention. He visited the palace daily, and was surrounded by well-wishers, influence seekers, and scores of others. He was convinced his lifelong goal had been achieved, and felt that his work was at an end. He thought he had won personal freedoms for the people of France; he sought nothing for himself.

The first sign that all was not as he imagined came when he suggested to the new king that the artisans and other working people of the country be admitted to the National Guard in order to give it a popular base that would represent the entire nation. Louis Philippe was stunned. "Arm the lower orders?" he asked. "I would be inviting my own ruin!"

Lafayette's disillusionment with the order he had created

was rapid. Three of the ministers who had served under Charles X were arrested on charges of treason, and Paris howled for their execution. Not only was Lafayette opposed to the death penalty on principle, but he was reminded of the Terror and was sickened by the prospect of bloodshed without justice.

His own position was made untenable when the National Guard was charged with the maintenance of order at the Luxembourg Palace, where the former ministers were placed on trial. Parisians appeared outside the palace in such numbers that regular army troops also were assigned to keep order, and they too were placed under Lafayette's command. He was in charge of 30,000 armed men, and if necessary he would be obliged to open fire on hundreds of thousands of citizens, thus precipitating the civil war he had tried so hard to avoid.

On December 12, the day the trial opened, he set up his own headquarters at the Luxembourg, and each day the crowds grew larger and more unruly. By the twentieth the people were in such an ugly mood that it appeared they might storm the palace at any time, and Lafayette went alone to appeal for reason. He was howled down by the fickle mob, and the experience shook him.

Early the following morning, a few hours before the verdict was expected, he made his last major experiment in democracy. He called the leaders of the mob, most of them university students, into the Luxembourg, and, explaining in detail what would happen if he was compelled to open fire, he appealed to them to keep the crowd under control.

The prisoners were found innocent, but while they were smuggled out of a rear door a rumor swept through the assembled throng that they had been judged guilty and would be put to death. The mob was satisfied and dispersed, and it is possible that the student leaders, impressed by Lafayette's description of the horrors that mob action would create, were responsible for disseminating the false story.

Lafayette believed that reason had prevailed, and was pleased. What he failed to realize was that by defending the ministers of Charles X, as the people thought he had done, he had sacrificed his own popularity. Louis Philippe saw an opportunity to get rid of the old man who continued to press for constitutional reforms, and on December 24 the Chamber, inspired by the crown, passed a bill abolishing the post of commander of the National Guard. Lafayette was made "honorary commander for life."

Louis Philippe wrote him a hypocritical letter thanking him for the services he had performed for his country over the period of more than a half century. Lafayette was startled by his sudden retirement, but had not yet grasped the significance of what was, in effect, his political epitaph.

Early in 1831 he wrote to a friend in the United States with his unquenchable optimism: "The march of liberty may be opposed, sometimes more, sometimes less, but the movement has really started, and our great work will bear fruit in France and in every country."

He kept his seat in the Chamber, and frequently delivered speeches on his favorite subject, liberty, failing to realize that much of what he had preached for decades had already come to pass. The new regime made no attempt to curb freedom of assembly, men of all faiths were allowed to worship as they pleased, and the press, although subject to subtle restrictions, was relatively free. Louis Philippe was gathering the reins of power into his own hands gradually, and in the process was building his own following by giving the people the prosperity and peace that France so desperately craved.

Lafayette was a patriarch now, a legendary figure revered by such liberty-loving authors as Victor Hugo and Stendahl. French and foreign liberals continued to visit La Grange in large numbers, and when Lafayette was in Paris he received more invitations than he could accept. The ordinary citizens for whose rights he had fought for so long no longer worshiped him, thanks to the Luxembourg trial, but liberals who knew politics regarded him as a near saint.

As he advanced further into his seventies he became deaf, and a stiffening of the joints made it difficult for him to walk. At La Grange he spent long periods each day meditating in the bedroom of his departed wife, and he carried her miniature with him at all times, often interrupting a conversation to gaze at it.

Remaining true to Adrienne's memory in his own fashion as he became somewhat senile, he was consistent in his attitude toward beautiful women. He never failed to notice a pretty girl, invariably kissing and caressing one who struck his fancy, much to the embarrassment of his family. Actresses and others of the demimonde were flattered by his attentions, but proper young ladies kept their distance from him.

He was consistent, too, in opposing tyranny, and when it became apparent to him, as it had to younger men, that Louis Philippe had no intention of setting up a real constitutional monarchy, Lafayette openly broke with him and refused to visit the Tuileries. "The King broke his word to me, and through me to the people," he said.

Early in May 1834 he returned to Paris after spending the winter at La Grange, where he had maintained his customary heavy correspondence. He had suffered from a succession of chest colds through the winter, but insisted he was recovered, and neither his children nor his grandchildren could persuade him to take the medicine that had been prescribed for him.

On May 9 he was caught outdoors in a rainstorm that sent him to bed with a severe chill, and in his weakened condition he was unable to fight off the complications that developed. He was impatient with his illness, angry because his body would not respond to his demands.

On May 19 the physicians attending him abandoned hope, and his children, their spouses, and a number of his grandchildren gathered at his bedside. Early on the morning of the twentieth he awakened from a deep sleep long enough to look at each of his children in turn. Then, clutching the miniature of his wife, he closed his eyes again and died. He was seventy-six years old.

The government issued an order prohibiting funeral orations or demonstrations. But many thousands lined the streets in silence and watched the funeral procession, in which 3,000 members of the National Guard participated. Services were held at the Church of the Assumption, and thereafter the coffin, covered with the French Tricolor and the American Stars and Stripes, was taken to the cemetery of Picpus, where Gilbert Motier de Lafayette was laid to rest beside his wife.

The United States Legation provided an urn of American soil, which was mixed with that of France, and the earth of both nations covered his grave.

Through the years millions of Frenchmen and Americans have visited Lafayette's grave. Since his death scarcely a week has passed without the mention of his name on the floor of the United States Senate or House of Representatives. But the true recognition of his life and his struggle for liberty may best be found elsewhere. Wherever in the world men and women are free—free to vote their consciences, free to read, write, speak, congregate, and worship as they please—they and their society owe a debt to Lafayette. Liberty itself is the permanent monument to the man and his accomplishments.

Select Bibliography

Bedoyère, Michael de la. *Lafayette.* New York, 1934.

Gottschalk, Louis. *Lafayette Comes to America.* New York, 1935.

———. *Lafayette Joins the American Army.* New York, 1937.

———. *Lafayette and the Close of the American Revolution.* New York, 1942.

———. *Lafayette Between the American and the French Revolution.* New York, 1950.

Lafayette, Gilbert Motier de. *Memoirs, Correspondence, and Manuscripts.* Paris, 1837–1838.

Lasteyrie, Virginie de. *Life of Mme de Lafayette.* Paris, 1868.

Latzko, Andreas. *Lafayette: A Life.* New York, 1936.

Maurois, André. *Adrienne: The Life of the Marquise de Lafayette.* New York, 1961.

Morgan, George. *The True Lafayette.* Philadelphia, 1919.

Whitlock, Brand. *Lafayette.* New York, 1929.

Index

241